THE DEEP YES: THE LOST ART OF TRUE RECEIVING

Dr. Rosalyn Dischiavo

Yes is a world, and in this world of yes, live...all worlds....

e.e. Cummings

CONTENTS

AUTHOR'S NOTE

About the use of pronouns: Because so many people do not fit into a mainstream gender schema, I have chosen to alternate the use of pronouns in this book between male (he/him/his), female (she/her/hers), and some neutrals such as they/them/theirs.

PRELUDE

What does it mean to say Yes? To know the joy of receiving without guilt or shame? How many of us can say that we use our bodies to do this with sleep, rest, food, touch or love? What would it add to our lives? Could it be the change that makes all of the difference to everything?

To say Yes to ourselves is a terrible risk. I know. We will fall. We will fall apart. We will fall to pieces. We will fall together. We will fall into love…which is the most terrifying risk of all.

And then…we will fill. It will start with a deep feeling of relaxation and rest, and we will fill with gratitude. We will fill with joy. We will fill with hope, and sweetness, and sensuality. We will fill with love. We will fill so full that we cannot help but spill honey onto everything and everyone that we know, and we won't care if they grumble or cry in gratitude while we do it.

We won't recognize ourselves. Our old self would feel foolish, juvenile, and childish like this. But, our Yes self, the wise one, knows joy and knows fulfillment and knows the release of years of tension, and will never give that up again.

There are many actions in this book that you can try. But, I'm going to challenge you--don't read this book with a goal in mind. I know that this flies in the face of everything you've ever read about how to accomplish a change. But, in the case of something as powerful as the Deep Yes, it's possible that in setting a goal, you could sell yourself terribly short. Instead, I invite you now, not just to read this book, but to *practice* some of the actions—even just one of the actions—slowly and gradually. They will cost you nothing, but they may change everything. *Practice* is a process, not a goal. By honoring practice, you honor process, and happiness does not live in achievement—it lives in the spaces in between, on the way there, or in the glow of reflection afterward.

This is what it means to say Yes. It means risk and it means change and it means joy. It means happiness. It means true strength. Let us begin the journey of Yes with our eyes open and our hearts as quiet as possible. Breathe.

Yes. Yes. Yes.

CHAPTER 1

INTRODUCTION

Twenty-seven young pairs of eyes look expectantly up at me from their seats in a classroom at the university where I teach.

"Which do you prefer, to give or to receive?" I ask. "Really think about this. Think about the pleasures of both. Be honest."

This is not a scientific poll, I am aware of that. I'm also aware that this is a Human Sexuality class, and that these students have discussed more intimate topics with their classmates than many people would with their best friends. They are more open than most at this point.

I pause again. "Don't be politically correct, or polite. OK...How many of you prefer to give?"

Twenty-seven arms raise in the air.

If you were their parents, would you read this with pride? "I've taught my kid right", you'd think. He's generous and kind. She's giving, not selfish. My kid's going to get along well in life.

There is truth in these ideas. That is, until we realize that you can't have one without the other. Denying either one is to deny deep pleasure. Denying receiving, in particular, is a recipe for stress, depression, and even addiction if we take it far enough.

My students are wiser than you might think some young twenty-somethings might be.

"I think I'd rather give because that way I have more control," one young woman admits. Lights dawn. Heads nod in agreement.

Many would argue that in the West, we are a world made of indulgence. We pamper ourselves with food, cosmetics, electronics, and household fripperies. There is truth to this, but indulgence is not true receiving. Indulgence actually comes from ignorance of how to receive, or reluctance to receive, and the art of true receiving has been lost to much of the world.

In the 1980's and 90's I read dozens of books about "codependence", "loving too much" and pulling myself up by my bootstraps. I had to learn to love myself first, the books proclaimed with authority, before I could love anyone else. While there were kernels of wisdom to these claims, there were also crucial pieces missing that led me on a sad merry-go-round. In the rhetoric of the day, we treated love as though it were a one-way road that you take *by* yourself, leading back *to* yourself.

Even if we wanted to, we can't take that road alone. It isn't built that way. In our commercial society, the idea of love becomes just another system of purchase and payment...you love me, and I'll love you; one thing for another. But, this metaphor is not a good one. It never occurs to us that accepting love IS love--that fully taking love in is the most loving thing we can do, not only for ourselves but also for the "giver". It doesn't occur to us that embracing love is, in fact, love itself. In the end, there is no giver and no receiver. There is only the received and the receiver, or both are denied.

What would your life be like if you made a conscious decision every day to take in? What if your practice was to do it joyfully and gratefully? What would happen if you consciously focused on receiving? Would you fall apart, become hopelessly dependent? Would you be a selfish person, endlessly centered on your needs alone? Or would you become an amazing cup that fills up and up and up, until it naturally spills its bounty out onto those around you?

I recently read an article written by Douglas Preston, who spent a week with the Dalai Lama in Santa Fe, New Mexico in April of 1991. It was before the monk became internationally famous, although he had already won the Nobel Peace Prize. The Dalai Lama spent a week in this beautiful town, eventually visiting the mountains and a ski area, claiming that it looked much like Tibet. A waitress at one of the ski lodges sat down with the group and asked the monk, "What is the meaning of life?" The Dalai Lama replied without hesitation, "The meaning of life is *happiness*. Hard question is not, 'What is meaning of life?' No, hard question is, 'What make happiness?'"[1]

I have made a practice of deep receiving for years. I find that I have become less and less self-centered, more and more productive, more loving, and *happier* by far. I believe that receiving is one of the lost keys to happiness. I would like to share some of what I have learned with you.

---

[1] The Week magazine, 5/2/14, Vol. 14 Issue 666.

CHAPTER 2
A HEALING YES

The Yes That is Required
The yes that is required is not the yes
of knowing anything for certain
it is not the yes
that creates something new
The yes that is required is the yes
that steps forth into lands unformed and wild
and says here is my entirety
here is my soul
It is this yes that the universe answers
in ways that change everything.

~Ann Betz[2]

When I was 20, I had my heart broken in love for the first time. The pain was an intensity and a magnitude that I

---

[2] Used with permission. For Ann's book please see Coaching the Spirit on Amazon.

can still recall to this day. I clearly remember the first night after the breakup. I managed to sleep, but dreamed that everything in my life had been put through a flattener. I woke with a palpable feeling of an enormous weight on my chest...a sensation I have never had before or since.

For months afterward, I dreamed of a nuclear devastation that had killed everything on the planet but me. The breakup had opened up old abandonment wounds from childhood. Some deep part of me decided that nothing would ever hurt me that way again. I wasn't aware I had made this decision, but I had. For years afterward, I avoided men I had any interest in, as if they had a hand on the nuclear button. I was at DEFCON 4, twenty-four hours a day.

It is impossible to shut down all romantic feelings without cutting off other feelings as well...joy, affection, even my friendships were deeply depleted. I avoided love, believing it to be the greatest threat to my well-being. I could not allow myself softness. It dropped me into a well that felt bottomless and isolated.

I was single for several years. I had no real relationships. Every once in awhile I would break down and sleep with someone. I carefully chose men who I knew I would never fall in love with. Because of it, I often felt guilty and wouldn't have sex with anyone more than once or twice. Even with the men I knew were only friends, I wouldn't allow the relationship to develop too closely.

My friendships with women suffered, as well. My hard crust was so seamlessly shellacked that I took the role of mentor with most of my friends. I never called for help, they called me. I was the strong one, the one with all of the practical advice and the therapeutic answers. I was the one who could see to the heart of the "problem". But, I had not a clue how to sit with someone else's pain. Sitting quietly would have brought me back to my own devastation. So I gave advice, I chided, and I bullied in the name of love. In doing so, I attracted some interesting characters. Women with a host of problems called me constantly. At one point, my three best friends were a bulimic, an anorexic with a personality disorder, and a compulsive liar.

Occasionally, I broke down. I would cry and cry and cry. I would confess my loneliness and my hopelessness that anything would ever change. I had some amazing support, despite my brokenness. One day, I was particularly low. My friend Rick took me out to brunch, listened sympathetically, then suggested I attend a retreat that was to happen in a few weeks. Against my own resistance, I went. I knew that I had to do something differently. I felt like I was dying inside. I didn't know it, but I was.

The moment I walked in the door of the retreat house, I saw a man who I had briefly dated in the past. He was coming toward me with his arms open. Still defended, I thought bitterly, "Oh, God, not *him*. Why did I come?" But, in the time that it took for him to walk across the room to me, something happened. I had the image of a huge sliding glass door in front of me that held all of my negativity and fear. Something inside me said, "*No*". And, in that moment, the door slid aside, enabling me to see this man come toward me, smiling, arms wide open. I opened my arms, and cried.

I cried all weekend at that retreat. I cried for what I had lost, and I cried for what I had kept from myself. I cried out the anger, and the hurt, and the fear. I was held in my grief and in my growth by a loving community, people who loved me despite who I was, as well as because of it. I could not have healed without them, and I could not have healed if I had not let them love me first. I was an empty cup. I needed the water they had to give.

I also realized that though receiving was vulnerable for me, it was not painful; it was pleasurable. When I look back on that time and think of the feelings that were in my body, the images of water are the ones I come back to over and over again. The sensation of satisfaction and relief that I had from finally allowing love of all types into myself was a wellspring, a canteen, a rainstorm in the desert healing the dry, parched earth of my heart and my soul. I was not just allowing romantic love after a breakup. I wasn't even really dating. I was allowing love on a larger scale for the first time ever, and it was wonderful, amazing, healing.

This experience has been a huge blessing in my life. I learned the truth at a fairly young age that, "It is better to have loved and lost, than never to have loved at all". The pain I caused myself in those years of being shut down was intense. It was far, far greater than the pain of the original wound. Since that time, I have consistently chosen to practice risk rather than protection, to practice love rather than to fear.

But, perhaps more importantly, I have learned that *taking in*, what I call the Deep Yes, is a rare gift not only to myself, but to everyone around me. I learned that my healing came when I was willing to let myself be vulnerable enough to accept love, support and compassion into my body, heart and soul. I also have learned, subsequently, that the more deeply I surrender into receiving, the greater and more pervasive my joy becomes.

I am not a perfect worker of this principle. In fact, I don't call it work. It is a practice. The need to remember receiving is a focus I bring myself lovingly back to again and again…and again. As in meditation, I don't beat myself up when I forget, I just bring my attention back to the practice, noticing the relief when I do so.

Why am I writing this book? I'm writing this book for myself. I'm writing this book for my loved ones. I'm writing this book for the therapists who might need it. And, I'm writing this book for some of you--the one who can't figure out why she's read 400 books, or why he's attended years of therapy, or why they are sober 15 years--and still feel stuck in the same patterns formed years ago.

This book is not another abundance book. Abundance is an important idea, and many books have taught us how to bring abundance into our lives, but what good is a feast if you don't pick up or digest the food?

This may be just another book for you. It may be one more step in the journey, or it could be a turning point--one where you move from the "Why?" into the "What" of things, from the pain into the ecstasy, from the tears to the laughter. This book is about pleasure. It is about love. It is about yin, and the receiving aspect of the Divine Feminine. It is about sex, and food, and roller coasters. It is about the missing link in our healing: being loved from the outside in.

CHAPTER 3
VULNERABILITY—THE SISTER TO RECEIVING

Vulnerability

That quality in people that enables them to be
defenseless, unfettered by ties of fear, unchained by ideologies,
unchartered by pre-determined goals;
powerless, lacking the will to impose or manipulate;
open, capable of being affected and shaped, reachable, gateless,
wall-less;
receptive, able to be reached and penetrated, unlocked, unblocked,
open-armed; growing, undefined in any final way,
in constant process of definition;
wanton, foolishly exposed to life and its crashing impact, free!

I don't know who authored this. It is posted in large letters on the walls of one of my favorite retreat centers in Livingston Manor, New York[3]. I copied it many years ago and I read it on a regular basis to remind myself that vulnerability is the only path to love

---

[3] Shalom Mountain

and happiness. I had to learn that the hard way, at first. But, after awhile, I let go of the "no pain, no gain" mentality and allowed joy and pleasure to be part of my process and my life, even in the toughest of my challenges.

One of the reasons that receiving is so difficult for people is that we perceive (correctly) that letting people in makes us vulnerable. Vulnerability is not something that most will celebrate; it is something the majority of people are actively afraid of. We do everything we can, sometimes, to avoid this feeling. Our view of vulnerability is often exclusively negative.

Yet there are payoffs to vulnerability. There is no risk without it, and therefore, no gain.

Hermit

I want to know if I have a right to be happy anyway
despite the endless tug of war with my womb and your seeds,
and the doctors ticking off counts on the baby abacus
as if the mystery is just a math problem.
as if the pain can be plumbed away
like another set of lonely eggs shed out without a date on
prom night.
when did blood become the central fact of my life?
how long since you have been to a sweat lodge?
how many years till we can enjoy another hot tub in
Northampton?
when can we reclaim our lovemaking—
our bodies, our lives?
five years? ten?
or maybe it is only next month, or the next.

and it is hopeless to stop the thing you know.
Hope lives all on his own like a hermit who comes to town
once a year for supplies,
you think he must be dead by now, he's never coming down
again.
and then he shows: battered, dirty, neglected and mean,
uninterested in talk or speculation.
and then you think surely he will stay awhile,
but no: he foots it back to the hills, he does, as fast as he
possibly can
and leaves us empty as a tin can, glad he's gone
and sorry he left.
--2002

I wrote this poem in vulnerability. In the early part of my marriage, we began a struggle with infertility. Little did I know that this would become a 10-year journey that never ended in becoming a mother. In the first year, though, I was still quite hopeful and yet very worried. I was looking, as usual, into what the meaning of this delay might be. What was I learning? What could I teach myself? What did Love have in mind, making us wait like this?

I was at a party with some friends discussing it when I realized out loud that I was afraid to mother because I, myself, having been raised by a single, very hard-working mom, did not receive all of the mothering that I needed. (I should add here that I didn't get the fathering that I needed, either, and it's important to note, because we hold fathers to a much lower standard in our culture than mothers). One of the women piped up very confidently. "Oh! Well it's obvious! You need a mother-healing." The women around her vigorously agreed and I found myself surrounded by friends making plans to do just that.

I look back on this and laugh, because my first instinct was to try to orchestrate the thing. A wise friend had other ideas. "No, no," she insisted. "You shouldn't do ANYTHING. You just show up. That's the whole point." The rest of them agreed and luckily I saw the wisdom in this and relented.

One of the women offered her seaside home as a site for the healing. The day of the event, I was to show at suppertime with no expectations. I drove down to the Connecticut shore, a place I have loved, and walked, and spent much of my life. The sun was setting and the beach across the street from the house was golden. I got out of my car and walked up the steps to the house. Little did I know that when I left that night, I would walk out permanently changed by the experience.

The first thing they did was greet me and take my sweater. Then, we all went across the street to a small beach where they told me to gather any objects that caught my eye. I did this in the fading sun, finding among other things, a piece of sea glass. The other women gathered things too, and we talked and laughed in a relaxed way, being easy with each other.

Next, they took me back inside the house and sat me down. They had created an altar and they sat me facing it. Then, they took places around the altar in a circle. Did we meditate for a bit, or pray? I don't remember. But, I do remember that what they did next was offer me objects that were precious pieces of themselves. One by one, each woman brought out something: a goddess figurine, a special candle, a small piece of jewelry. In some cases, these things had been occupying a personal altar or special space of that woman for many years. In all cases, the object was somehow sacred to the woman giving it, and each object had some significance about motherhood, being mothered, or the Great Mother.

My friends gifted me these marvelous things while telling me how very specifically special I was to them, and why. I was in tears for most of it, overwhelmed by their generosity and their love.

It was only the beginning of the night. When the gifting part was done, they fed me some light food: fruit, a bit of bread, some cheese. I was not to touch the food. They fed it to me until I was satisfied. When this was over, they led me to the center of the room, laid me down and took places around my body in a circle. I was to close my eyes, and they would do the rest.

These precious women spent what felt like hours then, lightly massaging me, stroking my face, caressing my hands. They touched my limbs and my hair, they did Reiki, and they sang to me. They sang and they chanted to their own Gods and Goddesses, sending me the most loving energy I had ever felt in my life.

The energy in my body became intense. I was humming with a vibration so powerful it became a shaking that I could not, and did not want to, control[4]. They continued to sing, to touch, to heal. My body was hot and it was cold. I was trembling violently and ecstatic. I felt a power underneath me like a well-governed earthquake or volcano, a controlled eruption of a Feminine Presence that entered my body and filled me with a grounded ecstasy that I will never forget. I was laughing, laughing, laughing. I was inhabited by the Goddess, inhabited by the Great Mother, Fertility Herself, Abundance Divine. How could I ever have thought there wasn't enough love in the world? How could I ever have thought there was ever a lack of anything? In that moment, there was more than I had ever needed. The More poured out of me and into the women singing, into the women healing, and they stood without

---

[4] I have since learned that shaking is a very important part of the process of healing a trauma.

my communicating a word, still singing, their song a crescendo of light, visible to me even with my eyes still closed. The energy in my prone body went through me as they stood, a great magnetic force that whooshed up, drawing my torso, back and head up with it off of the floor. As I moved, She moved. As She moved, I moved, and bright "light" came down from above.

Eventually, this came down. I have no idea how long that took. My friends re-seated themselves beside me, singing more softly, chanting into whispers. My body continued to shake as they slowly brought me back to the room. When I was able to open my eyes, I looked out onto a circle of beaming women, their faces lit from within. Everyone in the room had been healed by the experience.

I looked down. There was something in my right hand. It was a piece of sea glass. This small chunk had been in my hand for the entire experience, and it felt as though it had been put through a sacred kiln of fire. To this day, that glass is the most sacred object in my possession.

To say that this experience changed me is to say nothing at all. I was transformed, I was altered, I was healed. It happened in such a way that I feel full of this knowing whenever I need it: that a Great Love is there at all times, whether I remember it or not. I am a part of this Great Love, I have a right to this Love as a daughter of this earth, and to think otherwise is the greatest sickness of our world.

The Love that I speak of is the Joy of this world. She is the Divine Yin. She is the true feminine inside all of us, no matter our gender. And as such, She is far from the passive way She is often portrayed. I have heard many a teacher describe the Yin— the feminine--as passive. But the Yin is not passive if we define it as "inactive" or "inert". I have felt Her, I have embodied Her. She is power. She is creation. She is Love itself. And as such, she is the deepest form of yes, of joy, of receiving, of ecstasy.

Although I treasure this experience greatly, I don't believe that it's necessary to have a big event such as this to have a great transformation. In fact, I think that most people (including me) transform from tiny actions that we take daily. A small action practiced every day has more impact on our lives than any one big happening, such as the healing I describe above. Even five minutes a day of Yes practice will transform our lives in ways we cannot begin to imagine when we start.

Either way, if we want this ecstasy, this power, this joy, we must allow the other definition of passive in ourselves: we must allow it to *pass through* us, to come into us, to inhabit us. We must surrender to the power that Love has to make us happy. We must say a Deep Yes.

CHAPTER 4

THE YIN OF YES

Many people are now aware of the Chinese symbol of yin and yang. It is often depicted like this:

The most common modern understanding of this symbol is philosophical, and deals with the idea of the balance of opposites.

Yang, the white side of the symbol, is said to represent daylight and the masculine principles, which are in turn usually understood as follows in Traditional Chinese Medicine (TCM): masculine, male, day, descending energy, functioning (doing). Yin, the dark side of the symbol, is said to represent the night time and the feminine principles, which are usually understood as feminine, darkness/night, earth, moon, ascending energy, calm, structure (being). The white dot in the dark side of the symbol is said to represent the seed of light in the darkness or masculine in the feminine, and the dark dot in the white side is said to represent the seed of dark in the light or feminine in the masculine.

There are actually far more complex understandings of these concepts for the Chinese, especially those practicing TCM such as herbalists or acupuncturists, but basic ideas such as these are now circulating in our culture with little understanding of their original complexities. The symbol was, in fact, created very scientifically by precisely measuring daylight, the annual cycles of the earth around the sun, and the seasons[5]. This more complex explanation allows for incredible variation and movement between multiple energies, and therefore more accurately depicts the dance between many states of being, as well as non-binary ways of seeing masculine and feminine, giving and receiving.

Binary paradigms are part of our problem in not being able to receive. In the West, we tend to see things as black or white, this or that. Binary is the land of "either/or". We know on some level that there are many complexities, but we still act as though there aren't. In binary thinking, all things have boxes, and everything belongs in one box. It is our job to sort out which box. Are you gay or straight? Male or female? Married or single? Republican or Democrat? On some level we know that straight people can still sometimes be attracted to someone of the same sex. We know that babies are born with ambiguous sexes. We have seen people cohabitate without marriage and are committed without rings. We know that a Republican is not always a gun-toting Christian and a Democrat is not always a socialist intellectual. Yet we have little practice in out-of-the-boxes thinking.

---

[5] A GeoMedical Approach to Chinese Medicine: The Origin of the Yin Yang Symbol by Stefan Jaeger, National Library of Medicine, United States.

In a binary paradigm such as we have in the West, we are either giving or receiving. These things are seen as opposites, and there is no conscious understanding that they overlap.

Polarization

Polarizations are another way to view things. We see opposites, but we understand that opposites are actually part of one thing—two ends of a pole. If we put masculine and feminine on one of these poles, we would see that though opposites, they eventually come together in the middle, and are part of a whole.

Masculine   *Feminine*

However, polarizations are not always the best way to view these concepts, because opposites don't exist in a vacuum. They are more conceptual than real. Is a man the opposite of a woman? Popular language would have it so, but it's actually kind of a ridiculous concept. What on this earth is more similar to a man than a woman? Yet, there *are* differences in our bodies. Aside from our reproductive systems, most men have more motion sensors in their eyes and most women have more color sensors. Most women have keener hearing than men[6]. As individuals, these differences may vary, but as groups, there are truly many differences. Polarization isn't quite "either/or", but it doesn't allow the concept of "both/and" very easily.

In a polar paradigm, giving and receiving can come together in the middle somewhere, but they are still at opposite ends of a

---

[6] Leonard Sax, (2006). Why Gender Matters. Harmony

spectrum, and we have a tendency to lionize one end (giving) and demonize or minimize the importance of the other (receiving).

Integral Thinking: A New Lens

Integral thinking is a new paradigm that encompasses the complexities of our existence. We are not one thing or another with no overlap. But, we are also not simply some dot on the continuum of a line, either. The truth of us, and of the world, is that we are always in continuous movement and change: we are a dance of multiple realms of consciousness. We *do* have unique characteristics, and some of these can be quite stable throughout our lives. But, we also move and change, and each time some part of us does, everything in us moves with it. This is true of our relationship with the outside world, as well. When we change, we change the world, and when the world changes, it changes us.

Some of the students at my institute[7] recently came up with analogies for these stable, yet changing energies. They created an exercise where they asked people to imagine foods that they loved as children, but don't like now, and then to imagine foods that they hated as children but that they like or love now. They then asked people to discuss what their current orientation to food is: Omnivore? Vegetarian? Vegan? Carnivore? Pescatarian? No red meat? Paleo? The idea was to have people think about how our tastes, preferences and orientations to things change, some temporarily, some for a long time, and some forever.

In India, the idea of moving masculine and feminine energies, also have names and concepts. The God Shiva, who is said to be the embodiment of all consciousness, is the Yang principle. The

---

[7] Institute for Sexuality Education & Enlightenment, (ISEE) http://instituteforsexuality.com. Credit to Jolene Hamilton for the exercise.

Goddess Shakti, who is said to be the embodiment of all power, is the Yin principle[8]. Again, the modern or common understandings of these principles are often overly simplistic. If we were to compare the Chinese ideas to the Indian ones, Shiva would be Yang and Shakti would be Yin. However, just as Chinese medicine is far more complex than generally known, so, too is Indian philosophy. There are two additional and important forces at work: the feminine aspect of the masculine, which is called *tapas* in Sanskrit, and the masculine aspect of the feminine, called *spanda*. If we look at the yin/yang symbol, tapas would be the light spot in the dark side of the spiral and spanda the dark spot in the light side of the spiral.

Tapas can be described as a container that one puts on an action or a behavior. It is not the idea of shutting something away, but containing or holding a force or energy. Practicing an austerity, such as celibacy or fasting, can be seen as practicing a *tapas*, but so can changing any habit by containing a behavior somehow. *Tapas* also means "heat", partially because containment is a crucible that causes reactions. *Spanda* is the spontaneous, powerful result of tapas. It is unpredictable and unstoppable. Another word for this power is *kundalini* or *kundalini-shakti*. This power is the birthing force, it is considered feminine, and is said to be the only true power that exists. All consciousness lies in Shiva, all power lies in Shakti.

If we look at Indian theology a bit more, it is easy to see that these energies are not simple opposites. Shiva is depicted as Lord Destroyer, but also Lord of Meditation, and Lord of the Dance. He is often used as a yogic example of celibacy, but his Divine lovemaking with Sati for 1000 years created the world, and he had

---

[8] There are many, many different interpretations of this information. I pass down what was taught to me by my teacher. For more information, read *Kali Rising*, by Dr. Rudolph Ballantine.

many wives. Shakti, too, has many forms including Sati, Goddess of fertility and marital longevity; Parvati, a gentle mother goddess; Kali the Destoyer, who represents Time and Durga, a great Mother Goddess but also the demon slayer.

If we look at these energies in a modern light, we can begin to see that what we term "masculine" and what we term "feminine" are neither binary (one extreme or the other) nor simple. But, they have been represented more and more simplistically, and this has caused us many problems.

If, for example, we grow up in a society like the United States, we often hear the feminine being described as passive or nurturing. There is very little room for the idea of spanda, or power, in the feminine. The masculine is seen as active, or even destructive, with no acknowledgment of consciousness. There is little acknowledgment that each person is a unique mix of multiple energies and that thinking of these as opposites doesn't really work for any of us.

What does all of this have to do with the Deep Yes, you may ask? Well, the Yes is the Yin Feminine, the dark side of the spiral. I have had the Yin described to me as passive and nurturing by many, many books and many teachers. My experience has been somewhat different. The yin-feminine energy is one of receiving, of drawing in, of allowing, and it is an incredibly powerful process. The drawing in by the yin can be compared to the incomprehensible power of a gravitational singularity, or black hole. This may seem negative, but this is because black holes[9] are often feared and no one truly understands them yet. How very often I have heard someone say they don't understand women! Perhaps what they are

---

[9] Notice the connection between the darkness and the Yin energy here.

21

actually saying is that they don't understand the yin-feminine. This is undoubtedly true.

I am not a stereotypical feminist. I do not believe that we are in anything like the shape we were in when my mother grew up. Times have changed very rapidly, and though there are many feminists who do not see change and insist on various victim stances, many modern feminists like myself celebrate the advances we have made in many western cultures. We celebrate men, transgender and gender-fluid people, intersex folks, queer folks...we're all a part of the party.

However, I am not naïve to the fact that this is a fairly recent change in our status. My mother was not able to attain a credit card in her own name when I was a child because she wasn't married, despite the fact that she was gainfully employed and managed a home-health care company. I grew up with many boys who treated girls as inferior, and science and math teachers who rarely called on girls in class. One of my closest friends, who is my age, was made to take her high school calculus exam over in a room by herself merely because her original grade was very high. Her math teacher simply refused to believe that she was capable because of her gender and because she was a beautiful, vivacious, blonde female.

When we lived in societies that traditionally valued men above women, we also lived in societies that valued stereotypical "masculine" behaviors and characteristics over "feminine" ones. Unfortunately, many of these values were crystallized in unnatural ways that were never a part of a healthy masculine or a healthy life, yet they remain in our society today. This means that we value action over rest, we value productivity over contemplation, and we value results over process. The insanity of this thinking is obvious once it is held to the light. The better rested we are, the better we perform. We cannot produce without knowing what we want to produce, and results don't occur without process.

Despite recent advances and victories in our thinking, Western society is still very stuck in this value system and this leads to exhaustion, lack of replenishment and a depletion in true nourishment of the soul. The next chapters will look at examples of how this is true and discuss how to counterbalance these influences with the practices of the Deep Yes.

CHAPTER 5

ROLE MODELING NO

"When I was 5 years old, my mother always told me that happiness was the key to life. When I went to school, they asked me what I wanted to be when I grew up. I wrote down 'happy'. They told me I didn't understand the assignment, and I told them they didn't understand life."

—JOHN LENNON

Years ago, Professor Leo Buscaglia (nicknamed "The Love Doctor"), started a non-credit course called "Love 1A" at the University of Southern California. The tremendous popularity of his lectures, and books that followed, is testament to the idea that we are missing this crucial teaching somehow along the way. How we learn how to love has much to do with how we learn to receive—or not to.

The next statement here may seem obvious, and yet it is still unexamined: parents today have become indoctrinated into the standing belief that to receive is self-indulgent. Mothers give more and more to their children all of the time, exhausting themselves nearly beyond return. Sports practice, dance lessons, SAT classes, soccer games, all in the name of love and being a good parent, and most are also at paying jobs working full or part-time. When they collapse or break down, mothers blame themselves or head to the doctor for some pills to deal with this unsustainable situation.

Men have been indoctrinated into stoicism for the better part of 2 centuries now, where there is little room for softness, receiving, or relaxing. This idea has changed over the past 25 years, becoming less and less rigid. But, even more moderate, modern fathers are told that to be a man they must work overtime in a financially lucrative career and yet still be a good guy by being present and available for their wives and children. When they break down, it's time for a drink or a Prozac or a binge of sports on TV.

Never in the history of the world has the raising of children been seen as the job of one or two people alone. Extended families, communities, even whole towns have raised children. A child's behavior was contained by all of the adults in that child's circle. A child's informal education about life was seen as everyone's responsibility. In some areas of the world, this is still true. The modern Western world, in contrast, has technology that makes us *seem* more physically able to care for children ourselves, but in actuality makes us less accessible to each other and other resources.

Our friends, Janet and Jon, were progressive types who wanted their children to be able to stay home and play with the neighborhood kids rather than to be in organized activities. Their idea was that unstructured play time was more relaxing for kids, and had more potential for the development both of friendships and their children's imaginations. "Go play in the woods!" they challenged them, remembering the wonder they themselves felt as kids, creating fairylands or goblin fortresses in the glens of eastern Connecticut.

When they tried it, their children were alone. "We had to give it up," Jon told me with defeat in his eyes. "Everyone else has their kids in activities, and our kids had no one to play with."

This frenzy of child-centeredness is not good for children. In the book, "The Over-Scheduled Child," the authors state:

Good, involved parenting has turned into a relentless "to do" list...the media gives a nod to the need for down time, "letting kids be kids", but the agglomeration of all the articles we read and news reports we hear pressure us in the opposite direction. Barraged with messages from experts who tell us how to raise our children right, we well-meaning mothers and fathers end up worrying about matters big and small, striving to micro-manage every detail of our kids' lives, sometimes starting before birth.[10] (p. xvii)

Most parents are striving so hard that they don't realize the main thing they are modeling to their children is striving too hard. Do we really want to be teaching the next generation nothing about how to receive love, rest, replenishment? How do we teach it if we don't know how to do it?

I'm at my kitchen table with my laptop at the moment, writing, and David, my husband, is out on the deck doing the same. As I write, our 20 year-old neighbor is in the back splitting wood for us. He came to our door last week when the tree guy was here and asked me if we needed the firewood after the oaks came down. We offered to pay him to split and stack it, and he was happy.

---

[10]   Rosenfeld & Wise, The Overscheduled Child, St. Martin's Griffin, 2001

A couple of hours ago, I asked him if he wanted any water or iced tea. He shook his head and said he had brought his own. I smiled and went back into the house, and David and I continued working. About an hour later, David made lunch, and we took it onto the deck, in sight of the young man, and asked him if he would like to have some lunch. Again, he demurred, "No, thanks".

It makes me sad, this refusal. Maybe it's shyness, maybe he just didn't like what we were eating. We don't know him well. We've only met him very briefly once or twice before. My sadness comes from the idea that maybe he believes he is being polite by not accepting some small comforts from us, like lunch, or tea. Maybe he thinks good fences make good neighbors. I'm sure he is not being rude, he's just doing what he was taught, what was modeled to him. But, I wanted to make a connection with him, and now it's harder to do, because he didn't receive our small offers.

This small experience is one of many I see every day, of people denying themselves small pieces of love in the name of courtesy.

The No in Therapy

In his book, "The Heart of the Buddha's Teaching", Thich Nhat Hanh, celebrated Vietnamese Zen Buddhist monk, writes about psychotherapists, "Why do you only talk to your clients about suffering? Why not help them touch the seeds of happiness that are also there?[11]"

Therapists role model the "no" without realizing it. They have been taught to focus on the pain of childhood as a touchstone for healing. The theory is that if we understand how we were hurt, we

---

[11] Thich Nhat Hanh (1998). The Heart of the Buddha's Teaching: Transforming Suffering into Peace, Joy and Liberation. Broadway Books

can move through it. Many therapists unwittingly reinforce pain without knowing how to help the client to install love or pleasure in its stead. It is as if we perform surgery, see a tumor and remove it without anesthesia while the client lies in agony. Then we don't close the wound. The surgery becomes a trauma in and of itself.

I had a client awhile back. I'll call her Diana. She came to me for couples counseling with her husband. A few months later, they were stabilized, working their way through some issues, but no longer in need of regular sessions. Of the two of them, she is the one I remember the most, because of what she had to say to me when they first came to me with sexual problems between them.

"I was violently sexually abused by my mother for years," she revealed. The details of the abuse were horrendous. The troubles she had with physical intimacy were obvious results. But, the memory I keep was what she said on her second or third visit. "I keep remembering more," she cried, tears streaming. "I've been in therapy for 9 years and I keep remembering more of the abuse. When will it ever end?"

I felt very strongly for her at that moment. What she had been doing in therapy was trying to purge this pain. But, in Diana's case, there was too much to purge. And it was too deeply a part of her history to begin with a clean slate somewhere. Her problem was not ridding herself of pain. Her problem was that her body had no memory of safety. Her mind had a memory of love, but her core did not. Purging the poison was important, but if the result was an empty, lonely vessel, what would motivate her to finish?

"I don't think that remembering every detail is the point," I said. "You may never get to every memory, or all of the pain. But, I don't think you have to, in order to feel better. I think, instead, that you need an experience of safety and happiness in your body, alongside the experience of fear and pain. That way when you feel the pain, you have somewhere safe to go."

We discussed it, and she agreed to go on a retreat to explore this side of herself. Diana had never been comfortable with nurturing or touch due to her mother's abuse, but after two body-centered retreats, she had made a connection with safety and experienced a loving mother-energy that transformed her. She and her husband successfully completed therapy a few months later and, after almost 10 years, she came to completion with her primary therapist as well.

Diana still has issues. Her marriage still has issues. But, she is no longer stuck in a body with no way to connect with the pleasure and safety that will be her bedrock, her center, her heart in everyday life. The work she did was the work of receiving, not of purging, or merely understanding what had happened to her. It was pleasure, not "work", and it changed her experience of life.

The key to Diana's healing was locked in her body. This is the way we all must begin: in the body. If we are to take in love, take in pleasure, receive joy, receive healing, it must come through the senses. We must open the locks we have put on ourselves and take in.

The Exercise Push

Another perfect example of the role modeling of No, is in my experience of yoga in the last 10 years. I have always loved hatha yoga. We had a wonderful teacher near us named Bev. She was trained at Kripalu in Massachusetts during the time that Kripalu was an ashram. The teachers that came from Kripalu in those years are often treasures. Bev was definitely one of them. After each difficult or lengthy stretch, she used to say, "Now release and *receive.*" We would relax the pose and then be still and notice the deep relaxation that occurs *after* the pose is done. This is a very, very important part of both yoga and Tantra: to pay attention to the body and to pay attention to how what we do affects the body. At the end, we had a good 10 minutes or so of Shivasana, the pose that allows you to be still and feel all the benefits of a yoga session.

This practice is from yoga's original purpose: to prepare the body for meditation. Bev left the center awhile ago, and I tried to attend other classes there, but I couldn't do it. Most of the new teachers use a constantly flowing form which is more like exercise than yoga. There is no receiving. There is no gentle stretching. This form (at least the types I have attended) is barely yoga at all, as far as I can tell. I'm not knocking it as exercise, but I can't call it yoga. It's just another form of push, push, push with no letting up.

I had a great conversation about yoga with a young guy in his twenties a couple of years back. I told him that "no pain, no gain" was a popular myth. We can stretch into our pleasure and still have plenty of gain. He vehemently disagreed, and said that he hated yoga but still did it. I laughed and asked why? He said that when he felt tearing in his muscles, he always saw benefit from it in a day or two. I asked him if he'd ever practiced stretching into his pleasure, quite far but just before pain, to see if he had results from this. He looked surprised and said no, he hadn't. He assumed that if he wasn't hurting himself, it wasn't going to do anything for him.

Many people are unaware that the postural form that most Westerners today think of as "yoga" is actually a combination of ancient yoga philosophy combined with new twists on these ideas, British calisthenics, and Southwestern Indian wrestling and gymnastic traditions[12]. This combination was created by Krishnamacharya, who lived from 1888-1989. Much yoga in the classical sense was far more about meditation, mantra, sutras (teachings/scriptures) and a way of living life. Krishnamacharya was an amazing man who transformed yoga, but we should not think of it as ancient. Our modern yoga is quite new, and still changing. This is not a bad thing, but we should be very aware of how yoga is changing with our values and beware of teachers who use yoga primarily as an exercise of the body without including pranayama (breath work), meditation, or who do not let us pause often to receive our poses. These people are not necessarily poor teachers, but they may not be teaching us a yoga of the mind, body and spirit. Instead they may be unintentionally depriving us of one of the principal original purposes of yoga: consciousness via awareness of, and presence in, the body.

Not only is this a sad development in the world of yoga, it is true of many types of exercise. "No Pain, No Gain" is an accepted "truth" of today. Our exercise is now so often in gyms, by ourselves, while on machines and with headphones in. I can identify with this. I enjoy exercising, and it can feel like a relief to take time out of my day and not have to talk to anyone. On the other hand, I need balance in this area. If I'm not hiking, where I can connect with the natural world and a fellow climber, or biking, where I can do the same, I'm not as happy.

I think that we need both exercise for ourselves and exercise with others, so that we can take in the joy of play while making our bodies healthier. This may be one of the appeals of many Zumba and dance-type exercise classes. We can move our bodies while having some fun in a group.

---

[12] Yoga, Brief History of an Idea, David Gordon White, http://tinyurl.com/whiteyogahistory

Conclusion

To sum up, we are modeled "no" and "push" and "go" constantly. We cannot avoid it. But, we can begin to add Yes to our lives. We can look for solution-focused therapy that is strength-based. We can slow down our kids' lives to a manageable level and discipline ourselves not to over-control their activities. We can practice exercise that is fun and relaxing, as well as active. We can, and must, listen more closely to our bodies.

CHAPTER 6

THE YES AND NO OF ADDICTION

A whole lot of no can lead to an out-of-control yes. With almost 30 years of addiction study and field practice under my belt, I have observed that most addicts and alcoholics were once children who were emotionally neglected, left to themselves too much, had to take on too much responsibility for one reason or another, or abused. These constant "no's" as kids result in a consistent lack of fulfillment, a lack of skills to take in what they need, a "not enough" that takes hold in adolescence and adulthood even when there is no longer a deficit.

I began to understand some years ago that addiction is not merely greed, or selfishness, or an attempt to escape. Addiction is not the primarily inability to give, though it may certainly look like it from the outside. Addiction at its core is the inability to receive.

Many would argue this point, citing story after heartbreaking story of an addict's insensitivity to the needs of others, and they would be right. But, when we focus on giving first, we miss the point--the addict never learned to fully take in. The addict is some-one who never got enough of something in the first place, and continues to try to get what he has missed through drugs, alcohol, gambling, food--anything, in fact, that appears to give some nur-turance. Yet, like an old telephone, the addict's receiver is broken. She can talk all she wants, and others can listen, but when she tries to hear the reply from the other end, there appears to be no one there. They wind up feeling lost and lonely, unattended to, even as the love comes right at them.

Addicts and alcoholics are often wary of too much love, too much affection, too much genuine attention (though they often bask in admiration, which is not the same thing). People who are "too nice" often turn them off, or make them cautious.

Many recovering alcoholics speak of this phenomenon as feel-ing lonely in a crowd.

"I could be surrounded by people, in the middle of a party, but I would feel alone."

"If ten people were walking toward me and nine liked me but one didn't, I'd focus on the one who didn't like me."

Of course, addiction is more complex than this. Alcoholics, for instance, have a physical inability to process alcohol correctly, and this creates cravings for more once it is in the system[13]. But what of the alcoholic who hasn't had a drink in five years, and inexpli-cably picks one up again, knowing what he is risking? What causes

---

[13] Some alcoholics and drug addicts may also be born with lower levels of beta-endorphine, which can cause low self-esteem and a feeling of never quite belonging. For more information on this, read "Potatoes, Not Prozac" by Kathleen DesMaisons.

someone who is sober to want to drink long after the physical craving has gone away? What is the nature of the hole in this donut?

More important, how do we fill it? Alcoholics Anonymous has a program of recovery that addresses many of these issues, and it has been adopted by countless other 12-Step programs throughout the country and the world, but many members never understand what it is in AA or the 12 Steps that make it so successful for so many. Indeed, what is it? Many addicts and trauma survivors have felt the crux of the problem. "A whole room could be standing and cheering my name," one man put it, "and I'd be focused on the guy who left early to smoke a cigarette." Clearly, there's a puzzle piece that is missing in our understanding of what works to combat or counteract addiction.

Alcoholics Anonymous is an amazing program. It is, as members say, "for people who want it, not for people who need it." Almost everything about it is voluntary, from membership to how meetings are run to who runs them and how. There are no dues or fees for membership. The only requirement to belong to AA is a desire to stop drinking. All of these things are wonderful, yet it is the 12-Step program of recovery that has made AA unique and effective for so many.

It is said that when mythologist and writer Joseph Campbell was asked what was the most significant spiritual development of the 20th century, he replied, "The birth of the 12-Step program." Campbell felt that the idea that one could have spiritual growth based upon a Higher Power or a God of one's own understanding was groundbreaking. You didn't have to rely on someone else's idea of who or what a God or a Higher Power was. You could decide for yourself. Campbell may have been right, because AA's 12 Steps have been adopted and adapted for over 100 conditions, problems and disorders: codependency, drug addiction, compulsive overeating, debt, gambling, and more. Whether they are always appropriate or always as effective is not certain. But, the incredible appeal of the Steps is undeniable.

One possible reason why this is so is because: the Steps have a lot of Yes in them. They are not a list of "Thou Shalt Nots" or No's. In fact, there is nothing about what not to do in the Steps[14]. They are a lot about spiritual receiving. The Steps are full of acceptance, contemplation, willingness, surrender and getting help from others and from a Higher Power.

The Steps often take the member out of the realm of "do" and into the realm of "be". Many of the Steps use Yin language. The idea of powerlessness over alcohol raises eyebrows in folks who don't attend AA. They think that AA members are avoiding responsibility for their actions by admitting powerlessness. Instead, the AA member who admits powerless is practicing a paradox: by admitting powerlessness, the member can accept help. He can get a sponsor, pray to a Higher Power, take advice from group members--say a Yes to recovery. These things paradoxically allow abstinence from alcohol on a daily basis.

Other "be" rather than "do" language that relates to the Deep Yes in the Steps are "came to believe," "turn our will and our lives over", "were entirely ready", "became willing"—these are all processes of letting go, acceptance, surrender to a power greater than oneself, and ultimately, to spiritual awakening as a result.

---

[14] Not in the short form. In the descriptions of how to practice the Steps, plenty of advice is given about what works best for the most people and what often does not, but even so, the book Alcoholics Anonymous states that all of the Steps are suggestions.

It is not until the very last step, Step 12, that a member is asked to give back to another. This means that a practitioner of the 12 Steps is not trying to give away something that they don't yet have. They must practice acceptance, receiving and willingness before they are asked to help someone else. Done well, the 12 Steps reinforce a constant flow of taking in and giving back, taking in and giving back. But, they begin by taking in, by giving in, by surrender.

This is a perfect counterbalance to the Western world's frenetic insistence on performance, performance, performance. No wonder there are over 2 million people attending AA worldwide. No wonder the Steps have been used for so many other ills. It becomes clear that if an addict is someone who can't receive pleasure from what he is ingesting or doing, and does not take much love or energy from others or from any type of God or Higher Power, the Steps are one way that he could practice this receiving and be freed from the endless cycle of "never enough".

Of course, the Steps aren't the only reason that AA works, and they aren't the only part of the program that guides members to receive. The tough love practiced by certain groups and a lot of oldtimers is often joked about. "Take the cotton out of your ears and stick it in your mouth!" is a slogan used by harder-core 12-Step sponsors and members when dealing with a difficult or self-absorbed new member or sponsee. This blunt advice is another delivery method of the same message: take in. Receive. Say yes. Accept help, or die drunk or addicted.

Some sponsors will tell their sponsees to do everything the sponsor tells them to do or find a new sponsor. This may sound harsh or dangerous to the uneducated, but alcoholics and addicts are a stubborn bunch who often can use a kick in the pants in this way. By requiring this type of surrender, the sponsor ensures that the new member changes their behavior long enough to benefit from it. This is also called "Fake it Till You Make It", or "Move a Muscle, Change a Thought". Again, it is pushing the person to surrender, accept help, and receive. It is also encouraging someone to be embodied: change the behavior instead of just thinking and trying to figure it out.

People with other addictive and/or compulsive behaviors--sugar, shopping, eating, gambling, obsessively masturbating, video games—are also saying no to the things that they truly need and yes to the things that won't feed them emotionally, physically, intellectually or spiritually. Again, they need to examine where their true needs are, where they do or do not receive, and begin to practice accepting love, getting help, receiving abundance in other ways.

For people in 12-Step programs (Alcoholics Anonymous, Overeaters Anonymous, Gamblers Anonymous, Narcotics Anonymous, etc.), the Deep Yes is built into the Steps. For others who want to tackle the challenge of any addiction or a compulsive behavior, I recommend beginning with these questions:

1. What do I truly need right now? Not want--need? Is it happiness, peace of mind, time to myself, love from someone else?
2. Have I asked for what I need or want? Do I ask at all?
3. Do I listen when there is a yes, or do I always expect—and therefore hear---a no?
4. Do I ask the right people for what I need? Do I have enough people in my life to spread out my requests in a reasonable way? Do I keep going back to the wrong people over and over again, hoping they will change and be able to give me what I need when they have no history of doing so?

5. How can I get what I truly need? What steps can I take? What behaviors can I practice?
6. Am I in the right relationships to receive what I need?
7. Can I repair the communication in my relationships enough to begin to receive?

If you ask yourself these questions and begin to make changes in how you respond to your needs and in how you receive your Yes, you may find things get clearer. You may find that the compulsion to eat, shop or masturbate compulsively is significantly weaker, allowing you to get help in other ways and to focus on other things. These questions will not cure or stop a serious physical addiction. But, they may help you to move into more willingness to receive help from others.

The more quality people that you can pull in to help you, the better. Use chosen community, helpful family members, supportive partners, and good friends. Get professional help when and where it's available or join a support group. Remember, asking for help is a big yes to yourself, and it works beautifully. Most people wouldn't try to build a house all by themselves. It would take forever and what would be the point? What holds true for home improvement also holds true for self-improvement. You can make more progress, feel better, and be happier in far less time if you are willing to receive.

Conclusion

No matter what the addiction or compulsive behavior, you can bet your life that there is a big No behind it somewhere. The addict did not get enough of something vital, was regularly denied something crucial, or was neglected consistently, and then adapts this behavior into adult life, creating a pattern of dysfunctional and dangerous behavior. Our addictive behavior is our attempt to say Yes to ourselves, but since we don't know how to do this properly, or we go to the wrong things for our Yes, we are depleted rather than replenished. To undo the addiction, we must practice deep receiving.

CHAPTER 7
RECEIVING REQUIRES A BODY

When I teach, I often repeat this phrase like a mantra: Listen to your body. Listen to your body. Listen to your body. Many people are afraid to do this. We are afraid that if we listen, we will indulge ourselves. We think about those times when we wanted to eat 4 chocolate bars, or hook up with an unhealthy ex.

But, what if we didn't stop listening to our bodies at some point? What happens if we eat 4 chocolate bars and then keep listening? We will feel all of the negative effects of it. Better yet, what if we ate each bite slowly, savoring and paying attention the entire time? We would probably not eat more than a few bites.

What happens if we have sex with an unhealthy ex while paying a lot of attention to our body? We might have ecstasy while we are enjoying the sex, or we might realize that while we are having sex with this person, we are either overly attuned to their needs, or to ours. We might find the sex was good for reasons other than the other person. We might find that we allowed ourselves to be someone else, someone that we like, when we did it and then understand that this is what we were craving, not the person themselves.

What would happen if we paid attention to our bodies during exercise? Would we push it to the limits where we cause ourselves injury or put ourselves through pain, or would we find that exquisite stretch point that feels so good/hurts so good while we work out?

What would happen if we attended to our bodies' repulsions? Years ago, I was going to work at a job I had been doing for many years, and I began to feel as if I were dying each day. I would drag myself into the building every day, feeling as if the life force were draining out of me each time. It was very strong, but I kept going to work, because I didn't have enough money to quit, and I didn't know what else to do.

Finally, I told my then-fiancé, "I'm sorry. I know we can't afford for me to quit, but I can't do this anymore." He looked at me, worried, but said, "We'll make it work." I quit without another job, something that I never knew I was capable of doing. For a little while, I didn't work, I just rested and recovered from the strain I'd been putting on myself. Eventually I went to work for him, created a new billing system that allowed his business to thrive and added enough money to his budget to pay for my replacement. I found my dream job elsewhere within a few months. My husband eventually had a new office manager and I had a job in academia, where I had always wanted to be.

This would never have happened if I hadn't believed my body, which felt like it was dying, and obeyed the warning it was sending out. I could have gone the practical route and stayed in the job while I found something else, but I truly don't think it would have been the dream job I landed. I would not have had the energy to replenish, to accept the rest, and to contemplate.

This book has many suggestions for paying close attention to the body. One of my teachers called this "collecting the data.[15]" Whenever you do something you are not sure about, or try something new for change, make sure that you not only try the new thing, but spend time deeply listening to how your body responds to it afterward, and collect the data. It's not enough to know how crappy or how great you feel in the immediate action. Stay with it all the way through to the last effects of the behavior, and see what you can see.

---

[15] Read <u>Radical Healing</u>, by Dr. Rudolph Ballantine

CHAPTER 8
THE FOOD YES

I've struggled with food issues, literally, my entire life. Therapy and bodywork showed me that it began very early in infancy, before I could turn over. This hunger kept me captive for much of my childhood and adolescence. There was an inability to connect emotionally, a neglect of my feelings, a basic invisibility that I felt as a child.

I've been taught my whole life that there are good foods and bad foods. Of course, the "bad" ones were always the ones I wanted the most: sweets, fats, salts. Of these three, sweets have been both the siren call and the bane of my existence. At times in my life, I've craved sugar like an alcoholic craves a drink.

I dealt with these cravings for most of my life by denying them, but I also did something else that's a widespread behavior in America: I judged my food, and found it "bad" or "good". The judging of my food became a judging of myself: if I ate no sweets that day, I was good. If I'd had some sugar, I was bad. Authors such as Geneen Roth have written brilliant books on this phenomenon.[16]. But, what is this judgment all about? It's part of the Culture of No.

Food is pleasurable to almost every sense we have. It is pleasing to look at, to smell, to taste and to feel as it enters our systems. Sometimes even the sound is pleasurable. The apple is a good example. Apples are pleasing to the eye, and have been the subject of still life paintings and other art for hundreds, perhaps thousands, of years. They smell so good we flavor everything from candy to perfume to dish soap in their scents. We like the crunchy sound they make as we bite into them. We like the way they feel in our hands, and we love the way they taste so much, that there are now over 7000 types grown.

Most foods have similar characteristics. They are pleasing to almost all of the senses. But, the ones that give the most pleasure are the ones we judge the most harshly. And thus, they are the ones that we create a No for, setting ourselves up for an addiction. When I look at my former behavior around food, it is actually laughable.

Me (at work): I've got that last piece of pie at home, can't wait to eat it.

NO: But you had pie yesterday. If you eat it, you'll get fat.

Me: Oh wow, it was good! The perfect apple pie with the perfect crust. I haven't had crust like that in…

NO: Think of all the calories in that crust! You'll gain 5 pounds in a day!

Me: But, I can't just throw it out!

NO: Yes, you can. Be strong. Or at least wait until tomorrow.

---

[16] I just went to look up When Food is Love, one of my favorites of hers, and I found Women, Food and God by Roth, which I ordered immediately.

This dialog would go on all day. When I got home, it would resume. Should I have the pie? Not have the pie? Throw out the pie? Give it away?

By the time I ate the pie, I'd tortured myself with this argument. I would slam down the dessert in 5 minutes, barely noticing all of the pleasure it had to offer because I was so busy trying to avoid the guilt I knew was coming. Almost immediately afterward, it would hit.

NO: WHY did you do that? Now you're going to get on the scale and be miserable.
Me: But it was...
NO: You're weak. You can't even say no to a piece of pie.

The No could then continue to berate me for this breach of "morality" for minutes, hours or days.

What I'm commenting on here is a well-known phenomenon. The most successful weight management programs such as Weight Watchers allow all foods, not restricting the types so much as the amounts. This removal of the "good food/bad food" dichotomy is part of what helped me to lose 40 pounds and to keep it off for years.

Here's what these programs never taught me: to deeply take in the pleasure from the food I am eating, at the time I am eating it. *I am not just craving the taste, or even the nutrition I might be getting from some foods. I'm craving the pleasure.* I'm craving the Deep Yes. Allow the pleasure, and I usually don't over-indulge.

There are other reasons that we do not get deep satisfaction from our food. We have stripped much of the true nutrition from our diets. Do I eat apple pie, or apple flavored cake? One is full of fiber and vitamins, one consists mostly of white flour and sugar. The second is not bad, but it offers less in the way of satisfaction to our whole bodies.

In addition, there may be fewer nutrients in our food because there are fewer nutrients in our soil. The nutrition in our crops comes from the soil it grows in. Fields used for crops should lie fallow, undisturbed, after a few fertile seasons. This rest causes them to renew, rejuvenate, and to re-absorb minerals and other essentials back into the soil after offering them out to us in our produce. Farmers have been aware of this for eons, and good ones will rotate which fields are used in a given year. If the fields are treated with more and more chemicals and pesticides to force production, we end up with produce that contains far fewer nutrients than it should. Sure, our apples look terrific, but at what price for taste, satisfaction and actual nutrition?

Statistics gathered in the U.S. and The U.K. by the Soil Association show that levels of trace minerals in fruits and vegetables fell by up to 76% between 1940 and 1991.[17] What does this mean? When I heard this news for the first time, all I could think about was how much the rate of obesity has increased in the last few decades. Are we eating more and more because we are getting less and less out of each thing that we eat? This is not only true of raw fruits and vegetables. If our wheat is grown in the same manner, then everything made with it will have less nutrition, even "whole wheat" bread. If our corn is grown this way, the same will

---

[17] Coronary and Diabetic Care in the UK, 2004, James Cleeton, the Soil Association.

be true of every corn product from corn-on-the-cob to chips and breakfast cereal.[18]

Are we treating our fields the same way we treat ourselves, as workhorses who must be productive ("give") at all times? And what does this actually produce? It produces exhausted food that is less nutritious and exhausted bodies that are less efficient. In this way, it is possible to see that not only must we look at our receiving in an individual way, we must also look at how this attitude expresses itself in the entire makeup of our society, even how we grow our food. Our fields need not only to produce, but to receive the same love, care and nurturance that we ourselves must accept.

Solutions: The Food Yes

On a cultural level, organic farming may be a solution to some of these problems. It allows for resting the fields, rotating crops, and few or no pesticides. A quote from the soil association gives us good news:

"An independent review of the evidence found that organic crops had significantly higher levels of all 21 nutrients analyzed [sic] compared with conventional produce including vitamin C (27% more), magnesium (29% more), iron (21% more) and phosphorous (14% more). Organic spinach, lettuce, cabbage and potatoes showed particularly high levels of minerals."[19]

---

[18] There are many wonderful and important resources about food production and modified or poorly-bred foods such as modern wheat. Read the book Wheat Belly by Dr. William Davis or watch Food, Inc. or King Corn, great documentaries about the enormous changes in the nutrition in our crops.

[19] http://www.soilassociation.org/

For us as individuals, the good news is that organic food and healthy food is more available now than when I was a kid. My local supermarkets have large organic produce sections that I buy from regularly. I haven't stopped baking, or eating sweets. Organic flour is available. I like playing with different types of flour, too, like spelt, or oat flour. Raw sugar is another option. It is less processed and therefore preferable to regular white sugar. Grade B maple syrup is less processed, less sweet and more nutritious than grade A, and it's also more flavorful[20]. You can also get it at the health food store, online or at local farms if you live somewhere there are sugar maples. Honey is a whole food, and I use it with a little molasses in things like pumpkin pie. Some people who hate pumpkin pie love mine! It's far more complex and richer in taste than pie made with sugar[21].

Some argue that buying organic is more expensive, but this is only true in the short term. For instance, Type II Diabetes is on the rise to such a point that the Center for Disease Control terms it an epidemic. What are the experts saying is the culprit? In large part, a "western-style diet". The same is true for heart disease, the biggest killer of both American men and American women. These diseases cost us as individuals and families. They cost us financially because of medications, narrower job opportunities, lost work, but they also cost us holistically through loss of time with our families, doctors' office visits, medical equipment and less enjoyment of life in general.

These diseases also cost our society financially. The National Diabetes Information Clearinghouse estimates that diabetes alone

---

[20] Syrup is now categorized by color rather than grade in some places. The darker the syrup, the less refined and the more good stuff is still in it.

[21] I use the recipe on the back of the Libby's pumpkin can and I substitute mostly honey and some molasses for the sugar. I usually use about 1/5 molasses and the rest honey.

costs $132 billion dollars a year. The National Heart Association and the National Heart, Lung and Blood Institute estimate the cost of cardio-vascular diseases at $475 billion a year. These estimates include in-home health care, doctor and nurse visits, medications and medical devices and lost productivity.

In the end, buying organic food may be far less costly than buying non-organic groceries and produce, even in the short term. If eating one organic apple satisfies my body because of more nutrition, maybe I will only eat one instead of two. It is also one way to practice the Deep Yes when it comes to food.

Here's another. This is the way I eat a piece of apple pie today, when I'm practicing the Deep Yes.

First of all, I only eat really GOOD apple pie. I'm not wasting my time on some junk that was made 2 states away and is full of preservatives. I'll either make my own or buy it from a bakery I know that sells my favorite kinds. If I make my own I have the added benefit of knowing exactly what went into it. For instance, I know there's no added butter, which a lot of bakers add but which I don't need for enjoyment of apple pie. I also can put in exactly the right amount of sugar, honey or maple syrup that I want. Now I'm ready to enjoy it. Here's what The Deep Yes sounds like in my head.

Me: Oh baby, look at that piece of pie. MMMMMMMMMMMM MMMMMM. Look at those big pieces of apple, and it SMELLS soooo good. How much do I want?
YES: Start with this piece, and if I want a little more, I'll have it after I eat this.
Me: OH. GOD. IT'S. SO. GOOD.
NO: Should you be having this?

YES: Yes! Food is a great pleasure.

Me: Yay!!! Thank you, thank you, thank you God[22] for creating apples and pie! Oh, thanks, me! You rock. You make the best apple pie EVER.

YES: Why, thank you! I agree. I ROCK.

Me: Aw, it's over. Hmmm. Should I have more?

NO: No. Don't have more!

YES: Well, before we decide, let's feel it in the stomach for awhile. It feels soooo good down there right now. Also, why don't we stand up and see how that feels?[23]

Me: You're right. I feel warm all over. Yum. My chest is warm and my lower abdomen feels happy. DAMN, I'm a good baker.

About 99% of the time, when I practice this, I don't have any more pie, and I feel great for the rest of the night. The other 1% percent of the time, It's usually PMS, and I give myself a break for that. No worries and no regrets!

This practice includes enjoying as many aspects of the experience as I can think of: how my food smells, how it looks, appreciation of my own cooking, the feelings of satisfaction in my stomach and my body, and--very significantly--appreciation of me for letting myself appreciate it. It's the Meta-Yes.

Another very important tool I have found when eating is to take deep breaths after I eat a few bites. I have noticed that when I am jamming food down my throat, or ignoring signs that I am full, I am trying to feed something other than my stomach.

---

[22] I use many names for the divine, and I use them as they feel appropriate in the moment. My experience of the Divine is that divinity has many faces and aspects from the earth beneath my feet to a tree to a Loving Father or a Loving Mother.

[23] A HUGE amount of the time I don't know how full I am until I stand up. If I stand up in the middle of a meal, It often don't eat any more.

The Deep Yes, applied to food, is a deep appreciation of food. It begins with choosing good nutrition, but it also applies to appreciation of ANY food that feels good to eat. If you're going to eat a doughnut or a bag of corn chips, enjoy every bit of it. Eat it slowly, and savor every bite. Don't allow guilt to speak and practice thanking yourself for giving yourself the pleasure of the food you are eating. This inner dialog will replace the dialog you have about good foods and bad foods, or your "bad" behavior. This is a deep receiving of your food.

I eat bacon cheeseburgers with gorgonzola cheese. I eat corn chips with guacamole. I eat French fries, I eat ice cream, and it's not a rare occurrence, either. But, today I eat high quality food. I frequent a local restaurant where the beef has no hormones or antibiotics, and they hand cut their potato fries. I have a local butcher that sells grass-fed beef, which is much better for the body. (If you don't have a butcher like this, ask your local supermarket butcher if you can order it from them. Many times you can.) I eat corn chips made with organic corn, now available in all of my local supermarkets, and I make my own guacamole, which is very simple to do. If I'm eating out and I have Mexican, I like to go to the places where they make the guacamole at the table fresh for you, so you can see what they put into it. I eat Ben and Jerry's ice cream all the time. It's fabulous, deliriously good. The company uses the highest quality cream and other products, and they treat their cows with respect. Maybe this is why it just tastes better than many of the other ice creams on the market.

Again, the argument may be: but that stuff is expensive! My response is that I eat a lot less than I used to, which evens out the grocery bill. I am on no medications. I spend no significant money on coffee. I'm a normal weight, my blood pressure and triglycerides are low and my cholesterol is perfect. So I think it evens out in my favor, and I think the benefits far outweigh the apparent costs. For you as a reader, if you can choose even a few foods to begin buying organic each time you shop, it won't cost more than a few dollars extra, but could make a big difference in how you feel.

The other Deep Yes practice I like is to say grace before I eat. Some folks will pray to God to thank Him for their food. I usually take a moment to think of the animals that have sacrificed their lives so that I could live, and I thank them. Someday my ashes will add back to the environment in a similar way. I also consciously appreciate the plants and the farmers who have all contributed to my meal, and I thank the Universe/Earth/Goddess/God/The Great Love for all abundance.

You can try any one of these practices, a bit at a time. One practice each day for a month has a very powerful effect. Great meditation teachers have said that one thing done every single day, no matter how small, is far more powerful than one big thing or even many big things done every once in awhile.

CHAPTER 9
THE SLEEP YES

Sleep requires surrender. It's not something that we do, it's something that we allow to overtake us. Maybe this is why it's so unpopular in our culture. Sleep demands that we give up conscious control and let our bodies run the show, and many of us have little practice with this. In fact, it's not uncommon to hear people railing against the need for sleep, as if sleep were an enemy we must overcome, even though most of us acknowledge how amazing it feels to get a good night's sleep, and to have enough rest. We forget the pleasure and the promise of surrender, and all of the healing and joy that it brings. Sleep is a deep receiving.

I sometimes teach Health Psychology, and one semester I took a bold step. I assigned my students a personal health project. They could choose from a long list, but they had to change a problematic health behavior for 30 days. They were to research the topic, and keep a daily log of their feelings, thoughts and progress. They could quit smoking, abstain from alcohol, reduce sugar, take yoga, begin a structured weight loss, weight gain or exercise program, etc.

The students who felt the most impact from these projects and the ones who saw them as life-changing were the ones who a.) Meditated daily--which aids sleep or b.) Slept 8 hours nightly or c.) Quit caffeine--which aids sleep.

One young woman had been on anti-anxiety medication since her early teens, but by the end of 30 days without energy drinks or coffee, she didn't need it any more. She was baffled and angry that her doctors had never seriously asked her about her caffeine consumption habits. She simply had no idea how much of an impact caffeine could have. She was also grateful she had taken on the challenge, and had sworn off the substance with a calm determination that told me she meant it.

Americans are getting less sleep. I attended a national conference about sleep and college students a few years ago and learned that adults in this country are getting about 2 hours less sleep a night than they did a couple of decades ago--and we can't afford it. Inadequate sleep is correlated with everything from Attention Deficit Disorder to car accidents to cancer, and it now seems it may have a role in preventing dementia.

Our children, too, are suffering from less sleep, and poorer sleep quality. I used to marvel watching my nephews just before bedtime. They were maniacs. The more tired they were, the more hyperactive they became. I vividly recall them running crazily around and around my sister's kitchen and living room in a large, frenzied loop, laughing hysterically and speaking nonsense. But don't teachers report much the same behavior in kids they label with attention-deficit problems? Research shows that most of the time, the person who first "diagnoses" a child with A.D.D. is a teacher[24]. But is it Attention Deficit Disorder, or is it poor sleep?

---

[24] Sax, Leonard, Why Gender Matters.

Sleep is not merely for rest. Sleep is an incredibly active process, essential for the body's functioning. It regulates important timing processes in the body, enhances and stabilizes mood, improves cognitive functions and alertness, aids memory consolidation, restores and regenerates the body, and plays a big role in immune functioning.[25] Very recent research has found that when we are sleeping is the only time the glymphatic system is active. This system actually washes the brain clean of its toxins, and doctors are now wondering if chronic sleep deficit is implicated in Alzheimer's and Parkinson's diseases because buildup of toxins in the brain is a characteristic of both illnesses[26]. In fact, our body cannot perform many of the functions it needs to if we don't sleep, because sleep enables these processes to occur. Sadly, most of us are not aware of this, and equally sadly, sleep is part of the culture of No.

When I originally wrote this chapter, it was one of the longest in this book. This is how strongly I feel about the importance of sleep. Upon editing, I decided to sum up the issues, and hope that the most essential pieces get through.

The consequences of poor sleep are first seen in mood. Depression is the number one side effect of sleep deprivation, yet few doctors ask about sleep beyond a perfunctory question or two. To complicate matters, truly depressive patients often have co-occurring sleep issues. Doctors may assume that the depression is causing the sleep problem, rather than the other way around. Unfortunately for the average person in this situation, a prescription of anti-depressants is the usual quick fix, and yet the most

---

[25] Mary Carskadon, from a lecture at a College students and Sleep conference, 2006

[26] Published by researchers from the University of Rochester in the Journal Science, October 2013.

commonly utilized anti-depressants cause sleep problems. Merry-go-round, anyone?

Other consequences of sleep deprivation and poor quality sleep are found in performance. One study found that amounts of sleep were in direct correlation to college students Grade Point Averages (GPA's). The more the student slept, the higher the GPA. The less they slept, the lower the GPA. In terms of work and learning, we perform tasks better after 8 hours of sleep. Another important study found that people who had less than 6 hours of sleep performed more poorly on a task they had learned the day before, while those who had 6 hours performed the same, *but those who slept 8 hours had improved, even with no further practice.*

The immune system is also at its most active when we sleep. It is working overtime to protect us from harmful agents we encounter during the day. This is why when we don't sleep we are at high risk for getting sick, and why when we are sick we sleep so much. Our immune system is trying desperately to catch up. So, lack of sleep has both short-term health implications, and long-term. Lack of sleep for awhile may cause a cold or flu. Chronic lack of sleep may contribute to cancer or heart disease.[27]

Caffeine and Sleep

Let's talk about another merry-go-round as it pertains to sleep, yin, and yang. Caffeine.

"America runs on Dunkin." ~Dunkin' Donuts coffee ad

---

[27] Most of the studies cited in this chapter are from a conference called Sleep and College Students put on by Brown University a few years ago. But much of this data can also be found in a book called The Promise of Sleep, by Dr. William Dement.

"Have it your way. If your way is fast." ~Seattle's Best Coffee Ad

"The best part of waking up is Folgers in your cup." ~Folgers Ad

"Bring on the day." ~ Starbucks Double Shot Ad

Many Americans have become convinced that caffeine is a necessary part of their day. Slogans like the above both play on and create the popular myths that coffee enhances performance, speeds us up, or is necessary for waking.

We believe caffeine helps us to say yes. We think that caffeine is a yes to ourselves, to performance, and to a good mood. A little caffeine will probably not hurt most of us. But, the way that most Americans use caffeine creates its own need for more caffeine. It is an abuse of yang energy—an over-expression of the yang masculine—do, do, do. Go, go, go.

Caffeine interferes with sleep functioning. It keeps us artificially rousing (a state where we are not fully awake but not fully asleep) at intervals throughout the night. We don't even know that this is happening. We think we are asleep the whole time. This unnatural arousal does not allow us to sink properly into Slow Wave Sleep, which is the most restful part of our night. We wake up tired instead of rested. Then we drink more caffeine to remedy our exhaustion. The problem is compounded by the fact that we may be getting 7 or 8 hours in bed of this terrible rest, so we think we're OK and we don't understand how to fix it.

This cycle can go on forever. Most people in our country don't realize that it's not natural to wake up and feel groggy for an extended period. The well-rested might feel slightly slow when we first wake, but if we have the proper sleep, we should feel refreshed and good in the morning. I know people who have rarely or never experienced this sensation, and they find it hard to believe me when I tell them that I wake up every morning without an alarm clock or a cup of coffee.

I stopped drinking caffeine almost entirely in my 20's. After a few weeks, I realized something that I have been telling people ever since. *Caffeine makes you tired.* It really does! At first, of course, it enhances alertness, but in the end, as with all stimulants, there is the inevitable crash. I find that when I get into a habit of a few days of caffeine (for me all it takes is a cup of coffee a day), I am far more tired *all* the time, not just after a crash.

Spiritual Aspects of Sleep

There are even deeper implications for sleep deprivation if we consider some of sleep's lesser known, more esoteric aspects. Years ago, I read a wonderful book called, "Dreams, God's Forgotten Language", by a priest and counselor named John A. Sanford.[28] As a person with a lifelong pattern of intense and powerful dreams, I was fascinated with the topic. As a therapist, I have also found exploring dreams to be very useful in some cases when people are emotionally stuck, or their conscious minds cannot make the connections necessary to heal.

Sanford counseled people about their dreams for many years, and found them to be extremely helpful for emotional and spiritual health. In some cases, people's illnesses were healed. In many cases, his clients found peace and understanding after many years of struggling with difficult issues. Sanford takes a Christian approach, but many of his quotes are from the first five books of

---

[28] This book has been recently revised and is available for sale again. Dreams, God's Forgotten Language, John A. Sanford

the Old Testament and thus are inclusive of other religious traditions such as Judaism and Islam. He explores the interpretation
of dreams in the Bible and suggests that God speaks to us in our
sleep, through dreams.

In India, some of the most holy texts are the Upanishads. The
Mandukya Upanishad is one such scripture, and has many learned
interpretations. Among other things, the Mandukya Upanishad
describes four states: the waking, the dreaming, the deep sleep
and the Turiya, which transcends and includes all of the other
three. The dreaming state is a way to access Divine energies or dei-
ties. The deep sleep is a way to the ultimate Divine Source...and it
is this deepest stage of our sleep that we are beginning to deprive
ourselves of here in the West.

Modern science has recorded some aspects of these states as
brain waves[29]. We call them alpha, beta, theta, and delta waves.
Alpha waves have been seen in meditative and hypnologic states.
Beta is waking consciousness. Theta waves occur in our dreaming
states. Delta waves are part of slow wave sleep, where we get our
deepest rest[30]. But, if we read the Manduyka Upanishad, it seems
that deep sleep may also be our main way to connect with the
Divine Source, God, or Universal energy. It is essential for deep
replenishment, energy and the rest of the soul. Could it be that
deep sleep is like recharging our spiritual batteries, or refilling a
dry well?

---

[29] Many thanks to teacher and author Rudolph Ballentine, who taught me
these concepts.

[30] It is a fascinating fact that yogis often need less sleep because they experience
all of the waves while they are awake. Read The High Performance Mind by
brain wave researcher Anna Wise.

If we consider these ideas, then lack of sleep and poor sleep have many deep implications. Sleep deprivation means a lack of deep sleep, and therefore lack of connection to our Source. How can we tell what deficits we may have spiritually if we can't be restored and replenished with the Divine on a nightly basis, as we may need?

So, how do we begin to change things around if we aren't sleeping as we should? You can start by embracing the idea of sleep as a good thing—one of the best things that you can do for yourself. Don't minimize its importance. Don't see it as a luxury. It is a major bodily need. Would you treat eating that way? Practice seeing sleep as a wonderful experience that feeds, nurtures and replenishes you in ways that almost nothing else can.

After this, you can try some of the following tips from sleep experts.

How to Say Yes to Sleep

1. Try to keep a routine with when you go to sleep and when you wake up.
2. Limit your caffeine intake to 8 oz. a day or less.
3. Don't drink alcohol for an hour prior to going to bed.
4. Limit naps.
5. Exercise in the morning or the late afternoon, not at night. You can do a relaxing exercise such as hatha yoga in the evening but nothing too stimulating.
6. Try to get sunlight as soon as you wake up, and as often as possible throughout the day. This helps to maintain a healthy sleep cycle.

Good sleep may be one of the most essential things that we do, one of the best Yes practices we can have. For more information, read some of the books on sleep here in the footnotes and in the reference section. You will be able to feel your body say "Thank you!"

CHAPTER 10
THE BEAUTY YES

I use an exercise in my classes called "Cross the Line". It was created for teens in high schools, but I have adapted it for use with my college students. The class stands on one side of the room, behind a line that bisects the space. They are told that this is a risk-taking exercise, and they will be asked to cross the line if a statement that is read is true of them. They are also told that they are at choice to cross or not to cross, whether the statement is true or not.

I start off easy. "Cross the line if you like Ben and Jerry's ice cream." Most of them cross.

"Cross the line if you're secretly a Twilight fan." One or two young women sheepishly creep across the line, to much laughter.

"Cross the line if you watch more than one reality TV show a week." After each question, some students cross and others stay. When each question is done, everyone goes back to the start point.

Then the questions heat up. "Cross the line if you have lost someone close to you." "Cross the line if you have been sexual while drinking." "Cross the line if you have significantly hurt someone on purpose." For each of these questions, a few students, sometimes only one or two, will head bravely over to the other side, look each other in the eye, and then head back to start.

I always give the following as one option: "Cross the line if you believe you are beautiful." The last time I did this in a class of 16, not one of them crossed the line. I waited patiently, because sometimes it takes one brave soul before anyone will cross. But, not one of these gorgeous, young, healthy people crossed.

What is this? Why are people in our culture so brainwashed into believing they are not beautiful? Even those who fit the beauty standard of today seem to be blind to their own charms. Disorders such as anorexia, bulimia and body-dysmorphia are more prevalent. This used to be a female phenomenon but more and more men are developing these soul-illnesses and conditions. Young men in my classes often express deep dissatisfaction with their bodies.

At least as disturbing to me is this: what if they believe they are beautiful, but are afraid to admit it, sure that they will be looked down upon as egotistical or self-centered? Why is it OK for people to put down their looks, but not build themselves up? What impact does this have over time? Do we eventually lose our good body image, and bend to the things we say about ourselves out loud?

I have a friend who used to practice sacred sexual healing work. One day, she told me that women had no idea how much men needed to be able to worship their lovers[31]. She had many, many clients that asked almost nothing from her except that she allow them to adore her, look at her nude for as long as they wished, and appreciate her beauty. Tragically, many of them had had wives or

---

[31] She was talking about heterosexual people, but my friend identifies as queer.

girlfriends who would not allow them to fully appreciate their own beauty, and this denial became extremely painful to them. I told a partner of mine one day about this, and he agreed wholeheartedly. "Most women don't allow me to look at them long, or they deny my compliments when I tell them they're beautiful. It *robs* me," he said emphatically, "of one of my greatest pleasures."

Men are not immune to the other side of the equation by a long shot. Many men have rarely been admired openly, because our culture is not geared this way. There is a major exception for this in much of the mainstream gay male population, but gay men often complain that the beauty they are taught to worship is a shallow one, driven by media images. There are very few cultures in the world, in fact, that celebrate male beauty. This may seem unimportant, but it is not. Men want to be admired, in much the same way that women do, not because it "feeds their ego" but because it makes them feel seen, loved, respected. It increases their sense of their worth in the world. Unfortunately, cosmetics and supplement companies have picked up on this fact, and begun to market to men in a way that can decrease their confidence in appearance. Many young men nowadays are as obsessed with 6-pack abs and perfect hair as women are.

Transgender folks, too, struggle with these beauty norms. Male to female transgender people can have long, uphill climbs when it comes to making cosmetic parts of their transitions. They are taught, as we all are, that "women look this way" and "men look that way", and it can therefore be very confusing and frustrating for them to know which types of changes they want to make, and what will make them feel good when they look into the mirror. For these folks, attractiveness to themselves and congruence with their own self-image is very often more important than how much they appeal to others. In some cases, trans folks can be led down an endless road of expensive surgeries while they attempt to create the "perfect" or "acceptable" appearance as the gender with which they identify.

No matter what our gender, we all receive poor messages about our beauty. We often blame "the media" for this problem, but we should remember that companies who offer commercials finance the media. These companies make money by selling us things. If we are comfortable with who we are, we don't buy as many things, so companies generate messages (ads) that create false needs in us, and these perceived needs influence us to buy things--in this case, beauty, diet, and supplement products. The media is only a go-between. The real problem is that cosmetic and beauty corporations create campaigns that make us feel bad about ourselves. They know that if they create a desire in us, a perceived need, for a certain look, they can sell us their products.

The problem is that the need they create is bottomless. The impact of these ads is very powerful. They play upon existing fears that we all have of being unloved and alone. Then, they magically suggest a simplistic solution—a lipstick, a diet pill, a hair dye, an exercise shoe, a new "sports drink". This simple idea is insidious and it has a lot of staying power. It is so effective that my students literally look at me as if I am crazy when I challenge the assumption that they must feel badly about how they look. I can't count how many times I have seen people just shake their heads in resignation, bowing to the belief that they will always struggle with poor body image, and accept this as part of life as if it is a burden we all must simply bear.

<u>NO.</u> We can and MUST fight this awful, insidious problem. Beauty is a deep need, not a superficial desire. Superficial efforts to make our bodies attractive such as adding make-up, trendy

clothing or cute hairstyles are not wrong, they can be fun. But, they produce only glamour, not true beauty.

Glamour is a shine. It definitely attracts attention. My husband and I have commented that when you see a celebrity or a TV personality in real life, sometimes you can actually perceive a glamour around them. They almost look as though a light is shining on them all of the time. They appear brighter than the people next to them. It is not beauty, because their features are beside the point. I believe this glamour is why we call them "stars". To this day, I have no idea what this phenomenon actually is. It may be the collective projections of thousands (or even millions) of people onto the famous person, reflecting in their faces and their energies or auras. It may be that their success comes partially from their ability to project this glamour in the first place. I am not sure. Not all famous people have this star-like quality.

Glamour is not bad. Glamour is fun. Makeup, flashy clothes, sparkling earrings, a blinding smile--all can be a part of putting on a glamour. But it's important to know that glamour and beauty are separate phenomena. We can probably buy or produce glamour in a hundred different ways.

True beauty feeds the soul, not the ego. True beauty can be found in a craggy old face, a glowing pregnant woman, a parent holding a baby tenderly, a teenager speaking her truth, a person saying something brilliant and original. True beauty can be seen in trees, the ocean, nature, and the more we spend time in natural surroundings, the more beauty we absorb into ourselves. True beauty is something we embody and become, not something we put on, possess or achieve. The easiest way to appear more beautiful instantly is to wear a genuine smile of joy.

True beauty also includes shadow, not just light. The first time I saw Picasso's "The Rape of the Sabine Women", I wept from the power and beauty of it, yet the subject is very painful. This is true of poetry, theater and literature, as well.

The Beauty Yes

If we wish to be beautiful, we must learn how to receive beauty into ourselves. I have looked basically the same for much of my life, from age 20 to now, at 47. My weight has fluctuated and for several years I weighed much more than I do now. But, there have been times when I was heavier and I was complimented daily, and times at my current weight when I have gone long periods without a comment on my appearance.

I have determined that the difference is almost completely about my inner state. When I am self-pitying, depressed, begrudging, resentful or generally negative, no one seems to notice me. I am usually in these states because I have been hard, defended, not taking in, not receiving what is available for me. When I am jealous, petty, sniping or nasty I am ugly, no matter what I wear. I feel ugly, and I find that people avoid me. This is not beauty.

When I am happy, satisfied, glowing, alive and alight, people tell me I look beautiful. When I am deeply, honestly sad, I have also been called beautiful. Once, when I was angry and feeling empowered, I was called "magnificent". Our perceptions are not always about light, light, light. The outer perception that others have of my beauty is heavily impacted by the authenticity of my expression of myself. This is an important point, because many of us have been taught to project an image of positivity at all times, and this is glamour again, not true beauty. When we project in this way, all of our energy is going out, out, out. There is no energy coming in, no receiving.

How do we get from believing we look bad, to believing in and receiving from our own beauty? Like everything that works well, it is a practice. I stumbled upon this when I was in my early twenties. My two closest friends had both modeled locally. One was a gorgeous, full-bloom redhead with soft brown eyes and a wispy body. The other was a sophisticated long-haired blonde with tiger-colored eyes. The first was anorexic, the second was bulimic. They both were relentlessly critical of their images in the mirror. No amount of external reassurance penetrated their seamless delusions.

One day, while marveling over their conditions, something struck me. I did not have an eating disorder. But, I was chronically unhappy about my body, too. Was I as beautiful as they, without knowing it? Was I gorgeous, with an incredibly beautiful body, and not appreciating it? I suddenly had a vision of myself in my forties, looking at pictures of myself in my twenties, and lamenting that I hadn't appreciated myself.

I made a decision to stop making disparaging remarks about my body at that moment. I made a plan for myself. If I had a nega-tive body thought, or appearance thought, I had to apologize to myself, the way that I would to anyone else I had harmed. If I made the remark out loud, the apology had to be out loud. It only took me about 2 weeks to stop all negative remarks about my body. It took attention, and practice, but it worked. To this day, I have a better body-image than most women I know. This isn't because my body is necessarily any prettier, thinner, or fitter. It was true even when I was heavy. I just appreciate what I have as beautiful.

I am always amused by how many people listen to this story and worry that they will become "snobby" or that somehow their unwillingness to partake in self-abusive talk will be seen as a superior attitude, but believing that we are beautiful is not the same as believing we are more beautiful than others, or feeling superior to them. How many different types of flowers are there in the world? Trees? Blades of waving grass? Gorgeous animals of all shapes and sizes? You can compare a rose and a tiger, but you wouldn't make yourself choose which one was more beautiful, what would be the point?

Beauty Mantras

A mantra is a word, a phrase or a syllable that is repeated in our minds to create a certain effect, or to embody or know a certain energy. There are traditional Sanskrit mantras that can be very powerful, and I have used these for my spiritual practice. But I have also chosen small English phrases that help me feel beautiful when I am falling back onto the self-critical bandwagon. These behaviors are like meditation: I fail a lot, but I don't judge myself for it. I just calmly bring myself back to the practice that works.

One of the phrases I came up with a few years ago is, "I am living on the inside of beauty". This came from a CD set I was listening to years ago, called the Erotic and the Holy, by Rabbi Marc Gafni[32]. He was explaining a Hebrew saying that meant "living on the inside of God's face".[33] I liked the concept. At the time, I was struggling with some of the changes that age and my struggle with weight had brought to my body. I remembered how years before I had worried that I would be in my forties, lamenting my twenties. I decided again that I did not want to be in my sixties regretting

---

[32] **http://tinyurl.com/eroticandholy**
[33] This may be akin to the idea of "looking out through the eyes of God."

what I had missed of myself in my forties. I began to repeat to myself, at odd times, "I am living on the inside of beauty". It truly works. When I say this to myself, I feel luminescent. It has absolutely nothing to do with attracting others, or feeling superior. It is a recognition of my own light, which we all have. When I practice this, I find that people are more drawn to me as a teacher, as a friend, as a human being, as a woman. I am much happier and more at peace. It doesn't hurt that other people find me more attractive, either!

When thinking about what you can do to change your image of yourself, you can come up with your own phrases. Forget about how you want to look for a moment and ask yourself *how you want your body to feel when you feel beautiful.* Do you want to radiate? Shine? Beam? Twinkle? Sparkle? Zoom? Glow? Flow? Swish? Start with how you want to feel, physically and emotionally, and then create a phrase from this. "I am sparkling in beauty." "I am glowing in beauty." "I am flowing in beauty." "I am beaming in beauty." You can use different ones to suit your mood, but the more that you use one phrase, the more you will embody it, and people will see it.[34]

Discussing this with my husband, we talked about men and other gendered people and how they may see this need differently and feel this need differently. When he thought about his own needs around beauty, he was reminded of the Navajo poem below.

In beauty I walk.
With beauty before me, I walk.
With beauty behind me, I walk.
With beauty below me, I walk.

---

[34] At the moment, I am editing the rough draft of this book, and I decided it's time for a new one, as I've gotten off track. I'm going to try "I am emanating beauty."

With beauty above me, I walk.
With beauty all around me, I walk.
It is finished in beauty,
It is finished in beauty,
It is finished in beauty,
It is finished in beauty.
'Sa'ah naaghei, Bik'eh hozho
—from a Navajo Ceremony[35]

This is a wonderful concept that reminds us as human beings that we are part of the beauty that surrounds us. We are neither separate from, nor masters of, the earth and all of Her wonders. It also includes the actions of our bodies in concert with the beauty of nature. No matter what our gender, this poem can help us to feel part of, to feel present, to feel worthy and to feel powerfully beautiful.

Beauty Practice

Try the following regimen for one month. For the first two weeks, practice stopping all negative self-talk about your appearance by using the apology strategy above. After 2 weeks, add one or more of the phrases you have created, or use the poem above as your mantra. Mantras work more powerfully the more often they are used. Psychology and consciousness researchers know that the more that we repeat something, the more deeply it goes into our consciousness. We begin to dream differently, respond differently, feel differently. Repeat your beauty mantra to yourself at least 10 times daily, and as often as you remember it. If you pay close attention to the words, even better. This practice will begin to bear fruit more quickly than you can possibly imagine.

---

[35] *Four Masterworks of American Indian Literature*, ed. by John Bierhorst, 1974

The Praise and Adoration Yes

Did I say accepting *adoration* for your beauty? Your light? Your amazingness? You bet I did. The Deep Yes is not about thinking small. ANY amount of authentic loving or positive attention that comes our way, whether it be great or small, is worthy of a deep in-breath, an internal allowing of that wave of love to come in, and a verbal thank you.

So, how to say yes to admiration, adoration, even worship? Enjoy it! Practice standing still when someone compliments you on your face, your eyes, your hair, your body, your clothes, your style, your smile, your personality. Take a deep breath, pulling IN the energy of the compliment, and let the pleasure of that loving statement flow through your whole body from your belly to your toes to the top of your head. After you take the breath, look the person in the eye and say, "Thank you".

Conclusion

Beauty is a legitimate, deep need, and the appreciation and integration of it is an inside job. Without a vision of inner beauty, no outer intervention or purchase will make us happy. With such a vision, however, we are happier, our purchases are more effective and more fulfilling, we attract people like bees to honey, and we need less overall to make us shine like the stardust that we are.

CHAPTER 11

THE WHOLE BODY YES

Americans and other Westerners have become afraid of our bodies in many ways. In fact, this book is as much about getting more deeply in touch with our bodies, as it is anything else. One of the ways that we can see this is in our attitudes toward how our bodies appear.

OK, take a breath, because this chapter will seem radical to some readers, but I'm going to go there anyway.

We can start by looking at the far end of the body image spectrum: nudity. Why in the world am I getting into the topic of nudity? Why can't I just stick to the mainstream rhetoric about body image and promote affirmations, body-size awareness, and self-love? Why do I have to talk about nudity, of all things? That is so edgy, and unnecessary, isn't it?

Yes, it is definitely edgy for a lot of people. No, it is most definitely NOT unnecessary. Our BIG "no" to nudity in this country comes from our fear of sexuality, and it creates poor body-image, low self-esteem, problems in relationships and a focus on the exterior rather than our characters. If this seems paradoxical and strange, keep reading.

We don't have to focus on public nudity to make this point. We are more and more afraid to show our bodies to anyone anymore— our friends, our doctors, even (and sometimes, especially) our partners. We have even stopped looking at ourselves.

When I was a kid, the women changed together in the locker rooms at the YMCA, public pools, and clubs. At summer camp, the girls all stayed in the same cabins and we never thought twice about changing in front of each other. My friends and I regularly peed in the same bathroom when there was only one free. One person would go and then the other would take her turn while the first washed her hands. We never stopped talking the whole time.

All of this was completely normal. But, the younger generations seem to be very different. My students consistently report feelings of inadequacy, fear, and even disgust when I open a nudity discussion in my Human Sexuality class. Many of the young women have never even seen their sisters nude, never mind their friends--and their lovers? Forget it. A lot of them will not fully undress in front of their partners now. I co-hosted a radio show for awhile a few years back, and my co-host, who was younger, spoke openly on the air about how she wouldn't take her shirt off in front of her boyfriend while they were making love until they had been together for months.

People even have disgust reactions and discomfort with breastfeeding mothers. I have had discussions with folks who tell me that they think it is more "appropriate" if a woman hides her baby under a blanket while it is breastfeeding, just to spare them the terrible discomfort that they feel with an exposed breast. This reaction is directly tied to the fear of nudity, the sexualizing of the nude human body, and the fear of sexuality we have in our country.

This new trend deeply disturbs me. It's hard to imagine the kinds of consequences this has on our psyches, and it is reflected more and more in our laws. Public nudity of most kinds is against the law in most of the United States, except under specific circumstances. True, there are places such as some nude beaches where it is accepted, but these places are few and far between. Most folks raised in the U.S. feel that any public nudity is, at best, "inappropriate" and at worst, harmful. We are so convinced that nudity is harmful that this "fact" is not even questioned in our culture.

But, is nudity actually harmful? Is it harmful to children, for instance? Before I explore the research here, I want to first discuss my personal experiences with nudity growing up. Neither of my parents hid their nudity from us as very small children. Coming in and out of the shower, changing clothes or going from the bed to the bathroom at night, they were nude. I never felt any sense of inappropriate energy, nothing creepy, nothing weird. As we got older, my father began to cover himself in front of my sister and I, and my mother did the same with my brother. As far as our own nudity, nothing was made of it. In fact, we had a favorite game after we came out of the bath where we would race around the house as fast as we could in our birthday suits. I remember a terrific sense of glee and joy as we ran. My parents would laugh and laugh, and my mother gave the game a name, "nudie bombers". We were nudie bombers! We usually stopped when we got cold.

I give my mother high marks for something else, too. One afternoon when I was 7 or 8, the boys were flying around the neighborhood on their bikes, shirtless. I became angry that I couldn't do the same. I hadn't developed breasts yet. In fact, I didn't look much different from the boys. I decided to ride shirtless, too. I told my mother my plan. She hesitated, an odd look on her face. Then: "All right," she said.

I rode shirtless all afternoon and into the evening. I had a dual sense of both freedom and self-consciousness. The boys I rode with were at first a little awkward, and looked a couple of times at my chest, but then, apparently finding nothing remarkable, that was the end of it.

I never did it again. Somehow, I knew that it would be my last rebellion against the onslaught of rigid rules about how a female body should be properly covered. And it was, until I was in my twenties. When I look back on how my mother handled it, I feel that she did it perfectly. She allowed me to have my freedom, and also the experience of self-consciousness that came from breaking a social norm. She trusted me to find my own way, and I did. This was in the mid 1970's. Today, someone probably would have called Child Protective Services and reported her.

People argue with me that it's different today, more dangerous. But, this is not the case. In fact, the violent crime rate has dropped steadily and dramatically since that time. Our perceptions of danger have been skewed by a constant stream of horror stories from 24- hour news sources around the world. It used to be that if something tragic happened in our towns, we would hear about it. Now, if something tragic happens anywhere, we hear about it. The percentage of tragedies and horror stories goes up, but our immediate danger has, in fact, declined. Rape rates have been declining for many years in the U.S.[36]

---

[36] Bureau of Justice Statistics, http://bjs.ojp.usdoj.gov/content/glance/rape.cfm

What is amazing to me is that when I show this to workshop participants and students, they often will not believe it. They wonder aloud if there is less reporting of rape. But, there is no evidence for this. In fact, the social stigma against a victim of rape is far less than it was many years ago, when it was the accepted norm to blame a woman blatantly for her own victimization. This suggests that survivors of rape would not be any less inclined to report rape than they were in the 1970's. This is not to say that victim blame does not still happen. It certainly does, but the data is very clear: the U.S. has seen a dramatic decline in sexual assault, along with almost all other violent crimes.

Yet, we are more afraid of it than ever, and we assign the cause of it to things like nudity, but nudity has nothing to do with sexual assault. If it did, it would be impossible to have a nude beach without rampant violence and rape.

People also worry that seeing adults nude is harmful to children. When Janet Jackson had her "wardrobe malfunction" at the Superbowl in 2004, America was in an uproar over the fact that her breast had been exposed. The biggest criticism was that children had been watching, but children usually think nudity is natural, funny, or gross. They don't feel traumatized by nudity in and of itself.

Paul Okami and others have done multiple studies on the effects of nudity on children.[37] One of them studied children whose parents were nudists over an 18-year period to see what type of lasting effects their upbringing had on them. He and his colleagues

[37] 1. Okami, Olmstead, Abramson &Pendleton, 1998, Archives of Sexual Behavior.
2. Okami, P. (1995). Childhood exposure to parental nudity, parent-child co-sleeping and "Primal scenes": a review of clinical opinion and empirical evidence. *Journal of Sex Research, Vol. 32* (1)

found that parents being nude in front of their children did not harm them. They even found that accidental witnessing of sex between adults did no lasting harm to these children. In fact, kids raised in an environment where nudity was the norm and sex was treated as something natural, had better intimate relationships when they got older, were sexual at later ages, expressed more positive sexual interactions when they did decide to have it, did less drugs, and were less likely to steal than subjects in a control group who saw little or no nudity.

You cannot harm a child with nudity, unless your intent is to be sexual with that child, to frighten that child, or to create disgust. A child will sense ill intent. If there is no ill intent, nudity is not harmful. In fact, nudity is not harmful to anybody, and yet we remain avoidant of it. Not only do all states have laws against public nudity, but some cities and states in the U.S. have made *private* nudist associations illegal[38]. Just recently, a town in Arizona passed an ordinance to make it illegal for women to be nude in an all women's locker room at the town pool.

Not only is it important that we understand our social "no" to nudity, it is also very important that we understand what we lose by not—ahem—exposing ourselves to it. It is important to understand that saying yes to some nudity has wonderful implications and lasting impacts on our body image, our self-esteem, and our self-worth.

My Nude Story

My parents split when I was four, and I grew up in a single parent home. My mother was understandably anxious about my sister and I as we matured, and would often admonish us in a sharp voice to

---

[38] The Politics of Lust, John Ince

close the shades in our bedrooms after dark. She was afraid that a predator would see us and we would be vulnerable to violence. It made a lasting impression on me, and on a deep level I became afraid of men. I equated my own nudity with the possibility of violence.

I never realized how pervasive this fear was, nor how much it impacted my overall feeling of safety and well-being in the world until I was 28. That year, my friend Janice moved from Connecticut to New Mexico. All of her belongings had to make it cross country, and she managed to plan to get everything across in one trip except one thing—a 1972 VW magic microbus, complete with vintage orange flowered curtains—a hippie's dream. I offered to take it to Albuquerque for her, and she gratefully agreed. I found my traveling companion, a friend named Sue whose teaching job left her free for the summer. I taught her how to drive a stick-shift on a 23 year-old bus with no second gear. The bus had to be driven gingerly and the name stuck, so Ginger it was.

Together, we completed a great American tradition: the cross-country road trip. Sue and I had a lot of fun, and we both grew in interesting ways. I was a counselor in a drug and alcohol clinic at the time, and she was a middle-school teacher. In the beginning of the trip, my casual use of profanity shocked her. By the end of it, she was spewing a blue streak at a bus driver in Flagstaff who started up his mechanical behemoth at 5 in the morning in our campground, waking her sleep-deprived body.

When we first reached Albuquerque, we rested. A day or two later, Janice took us up into the Jemez mountains. We parked Ginger and set up camp at a small spot in the pines where some other folks had gathered. It grew dark and we took towels and climbed up a path until we reached our destination--hot springs. The water came out scalding, but cascaded down the mountain and was caught in several small pools, each lower one successively cooler than the last.

We undressed in the light of the moon. Several other bathers were there already, all nude. I was very nervous at first, but I felt a sense of magic and wonder as I stepped into the rock pool under the night sky, smelling fir trees and hearing nothing but the whispers of the pines and sometimes a respectfully low murmur from one bather to another. There were men and women present. Most of us were young. I was aware I was naked, I knew I was being seen, and yet once I looked around and became present, I felt a sense of safety I had never felt before in my life. Here I was, nude in front of strange men. It was everything I had ever been told to be afraid of. It was also the most spiritual, sensual and joyful moment I had ever known.

As I spent the next hour or two in the springs, moving from one pool to another, I barely spoke a word. I remember gliding to the edge of a rock wall that held the water and looking down on a narrow valley. The moon was rising over my right shoulder, shining its light on the trees on the other side. It is a moment I will never forget.

Janice, Sue, and I eventually headed back down the mountain. We spent the night sleeping in Ginger and a small tent, and in the morning headed up to the springs again. But, that morning, the bathers wore swimsuits and made noise. Some people were getting high, some were rough-housing in the pools. We decided to leave the springs and walked down to a river on the floor of the valley. There were large meadows on either side. Janice told us she was getting naked so she could swim. She stripped and walked into the river. This was a different challenge for me than it had been the night before. It was broad daylight. There were no other nude bathers. Anyone could come at any time. Sue and I looked at each other. We were New England raised girls, Puritanism bred into our bones.

We went for it. Got naked again, and slid right into the river. This time we made noise. We had Janice's dog Blake with us, and he loved to swim. Problem was, he also loved to stir up the silt on the river bottom, and before we knew it we were all covered in mud, laughing till our sides split. When we got out, I saw a man headed our way across the field with a fishing pole. He did an obvious double take, took a brief second or two to soak in the vision of 3 young women with no clothes, and politely turned around, not looking back. A few minutes later, another guy did the same thing.

These two encounters meant at least as much to me as what had happened the night before. They shifted the message in the cells of my body from "men are dangerous" to "some men are dangerous, but most aren't". I also felt a shift in how I felt about how my body looked. I had felt seen in a lovely way, both in the night-time and in the day. I felt supported in my body. It felt erotic and beautiful and loving. This shift would not have happened had I not been nude. These shifts were made possible *because* I was nude.

I have never been the same since that time. I have felt more open, more alive, more love for myself and more ease in *every aspect of my life* from that moment on. It is difficult to express how pervasive this fear is in us, and how many benefits can be had by facing it.

It was years before I was publicly nude again, but once I did find an appropriate place for it, I have made it a practice. I attend clothing-optional retreats, go to clothing optional places, and feel freer than most people do in their bodies. I know my body to be beautiful, not because I am beautiful but because we all are. When we are exposed to the full bodies of others, we no longer compare ourselves to Photo-Shopped models. We know how much variety exists, and we can appreciate ourselves for our wild and exotic blends of shapes, colors, sizes, curves, and textures.

Another immeasurably valuable privilege of taking this risk is to have the experience of being with other women who see their own beauty because of this practice. I have met very large women, women in their 70's and 80's, women with blemishes, or mastectomies, all of whom are happy and proud of their bodies. I can't stress enough: they aren't nude because they are proud. They are proud because nudity has made them that way. It is beyond delightful to have conversations with women that don't include the neuroses of poor body image. All of the energy normally wasted toward this obsession can be directed toward much more important things.

Many men feel similarly. I have heard men say that they feel much more natural when nude, much freer in their bodies and their lives. They are less penis-focused (many men have fears about the size or shape of their penises) and more present in their bodies. Contrary to many people's fears, there are very few "creepy" people in clothing-optional environments. Predators do not like to spend time where everything is natural and exposed. They prefer secrecy and the dark. The very openness of these places drives most "creeps"[39] away.

When we practice nudity occasionally or regularly, we get another benefit, as well. We stop seeing nudity as automatically

---

[39] If you think about the very word "creep", it gives this away by suggesting that the person must sneak around in the dark.

connected to sexuality. In America, seeing someone nude usually means sex is about to happen, whether it's live or onscreen. *But separating these two things allows sexuality to be freer from concerns about how we look.* It allows us to focus on how our body *feels*, rather than how it looks, and how our sexual partners feel. This leads to much less self-centeredness in the bedroom, and that leads to better sex.

What are some ways to begin to say yes to the full (or at least fuller) exposure of our bodies? How about:

- Wearing clothes that show more of our bodies without worrying if we can "get away with it"?
- Changing in front of friends?
- Going to the beach without shawls and cover-ups?
- Going to a nude beach or resort?
- Taking a clothing-optional workshop?
- Looking at websites such as The Century Project[40] or Betty Dodson's[41] art galleries, where all types of real, non-altered, nude bodies of all genders are shown?
- Leaving the light on when we make love?

One of the students at my institute is a young woman who is a practicing sex educator in Toronto. She has weekly group meetings with other women, and no matter what the topic, they are nude for the duration. Their purpose was to get more comfortable with themselves and their bodies, and she reports that it is working very well. Anyone can start a group this way, it only takes a few interested folks and a private place. I know of several Native American-style sweat-lodge ceremonies that happen on a regular basis, and are held nude with only men. These new forms of the sweat-lodges have been adapted from ancient traditions and

---

[40] www.thecenturyproject.com
[41] www.dodsonandross.com

can be deeply meaningful for the men involved. Many traditional folks, too, have opened their minds and ceremonies to those of all genders, including women and transgender people, with great results and a deepening of the experience for all.

We do not have to be nude in public for healing to take place. We can also practice being entirely nude in front of our partners, and fully allowing them to look at us from head to toe without quickly jumping into bed or turning off the lights. We can stay present through the awkward feelings we may have at first, and say "thank you", if they compliment us on any aspect of our bodies. If this is hard, remember to breathe through the process. You can tell your partner it is hard for you, and let them know what you are trying to do. They may appreciate the information. I have yet to meet a decent human being who would not be happy to help a love or sex partner in this way.

No matter how we manage it, it's an important step to try being nude with others once in awhile (or often) in a non-sexual setting. This could be with our partners, our families, or with others. When we begin to uncover our bodies, we also uncover a deep sense of self-acceptance and self-love that is not possible in such depth and breadth any other way.

CHAPTER 12
THE TOUCH YES

Touch is a very tender topic, and it's a huge one for the discussion of The Deep Yes. We begin life with the most touch we will ever receive. In the womb, we are held at all times by walls of warm skin encircling us. When we are babies, we are passed from set of arms to set of arms, and those who hold us do so at chest level-- we can feel their heartbeats.

As we become toddlers, many of us still approach any adult fearlessly, trusting that arms will hold us; that if we run at someone full speed, they will catch us and then help us on our way. As small children, too, we run into each other, we play with each other, we wrestle each other, we hug one another.

We know from research that the more touch we get, the happier and healthier we are, no matter our age, but the older we get, the less touch we receive, and the less we give. We also know that children laugh far more often than teenagers, and teens laugh far more often than adults. I wonder if these two things are correlated, laughter and touch. Perhaps our joy is reduced as our need for warmth and connection gets more severe due to this reduction in healthy human contact.

Children receive most of the touch in our society, and once we reach puberty, fears of "inappropriate" touch and feelings cause those who love us to back away, "toughening up" the boys and "protecting" the girls. We receive these messages both consciously and unconsciously, directly and indirectly, and we begin to fear touching our friends for being misunderstood, we begin to fear touching strangers for being misinterpreted. Most of us will emulate the adults around us whether we realize it or not.

We receive less and less touch as we move into adolescence. As a sex educator, I have often wondered if our touch-phobic culture leads to a higher incidence of earlier sexual involvement. Many parents worry if their teenage sons or daughters are snuggling a little too close to their current sweetie, concerned this may lead to sex. Shouldn't we also worry that skin hunger from this gradual decaying of familial and friendly touch might cause our kids to seek sex as the only accessible form of it?

Two of the chief causes of our cultural touch-phobia come from related issues: the fusion of perceptions of touch with sexuality, and the fears and negative attitudes we have about sex.

Let's deal with the first issue: the fusion of sex and touch. In western culture, we have merged these two things as if they were one. The issue is far bigger than is at first evident. We actually confuse all eroticism with sexuality, and this has enormous implications for our happiness and health.

Rabbi Marc Gafni talks about the exile of the erotic into the sexual[42]. He says that we have unconsciously confined all of our erotic pleasure--i.e. food, touch, appreciation of beauty-- into the realm of sexuality. This is backward. Sexuality is a subset of

---

[42] The Erotic and the Holy, Marc Gafni

eroticism, not the other way around. Before we discuss the problems that this causes, let's look at how this shows up.

Have you ever called a decadent dessert orgasmic? How about sinful, or naughty? How many times have you heard someone say, "This chocolate is like sex"? You can insert all kinds of other pleasures here: the warm sun after a long winter on your skin, isn't that like sex? People have used this phrase to describe everything from smooth surfaces to rides in fancy cars.

Often it brings a laugh when someone does. To say that a sensual experience is like sex is funny because we feel some truth in that. This brings in the second prong of the issues mentioned above: the fear of sexuality and our negative cultural attitudes about it. What we don't realize is that we've been conditioned to think that erotic pleasure is sexual pleasure, and we've been taught that sexual pleasure is wrong, or only to be had in a very particular set of circumstances. When we laugh, that's because our often-guilty internal child is having some fun with breaking the rules.

When we are kids, we haven't yet been taught how to cut our pleasure into sections. We enjoy everything with whole hearts, whole bodies, whole minds. In the 1940's, a researcher gathered data about what caused erections in younger boys, and they discovered it was everything from sitting in warm sand to singing the national anthem to setting a field on fire. When I show this statistic to groups, they are often baffled or amused, and in some cases, offended. But, this data is very important because it shows that at that age, boys have a whole-body experience of excitement. When something exciting happens, their entire system responds. Here's the kicker, though--this is not something that we should want to grow out of.

At some stage, parents and society will begin to teach that boy (and of course, girls too) that sexual feelings are wrong, bad or--my favorite new millennium shame word--"inappropriate". This doesn't always happen consciously. The child just picks up negative information. As we do, we begin to cut ourselves off from the sensual and lovely feelings in the lower parts of our bodies, even if our experience is not a sexual one. As we do, we lessen our natural ability to feel anything at all with true fullness, we deaden our overall sensations, deaden our life force, dull our pleasure in everything, without even realizing it is happening.

So you see, our inability to receive touch or to appreciate it has very deep roots, and very broad consequences.

I want to share this story. I was a member of a support group for teenagers with family troubles. We met in the activity room of a church once a week. We had great mentors. One day, someone brought in a copy of A Warm Fuzzy Tale, a wonderful book for children of all ages[43]. It tells a story of how generous, kind and giving people became fearful, sick and mean because they became convinced of the lie that love was in limited supply, and if they gave too much away they might run out.

We were teenagers. We loved the story, and part of what we talked about was our desire for touch. We began to brush each other's hair or rub each other's backs during our meetings. This was a clean, innocent and lovely gift in my life. I could receive touch without worrying about what it meant, without feeling I owed someone something, without confusing it with sex. I could give touch freely, too, which was a tremendous blessing in itself. I learned how much joy you can truly give someone just from a stroke on their arm, or some pats on their back. As a very depressed teen, I believe it

---

[43] A Warm Fuzzy Tale, Claude Steiner & Jo Ann Dick

may have saved my life to have this outlet for my desire to give and receive love, and to feel wanted and needed by this compassionate and exceptional group of my peers.

Every once in awhile, someone from the church where we met would walk through the room our meeting was held. This was in and of itself a problem, since it was supposed to be an anonymous support group (we weren't associated with the church) where we could feel safe talking about our feelings and our problems without interference. We soon learned that the people who had passed through our meeting room had complained that we looked like we were "having an orgy". This was despite the fact that we never felt or looked guilty, never stopped what we were doing when someone came into the room, never touched each other sexually, and were always fully dressed.

No one gave us a chance to explain, or if they did, they didn't like the explanation. They asked us to leave. We had to find another space to meet.

I really don't harbor a grudge against the people of that church. They were raised in an erotophobic society where touch meant sex or abuse. They were operating in a litigious society, too. Perhaps they were afraid that they would be sued if someone took offense to the touch and complained. But, it was remarkable how The Warm Fuzzy story suddenly came to life. All of the fears, meanness and contraction that the book described unrolled in front of us in a living color illustration of this cautionary tale.

We didn't hold resentment. We knew what had happened, we had seen with our own eyes how fear of "not enough" had almost been a tragic damper on the warmth of our group. To this day, I thank God that the adult mentors of this group did not follow their own fears of being misunderstood[44]. They never told us we might want to reconsider our touching, they just found us another place to meet.

This experience was formative for me. I do not touch people without their permission, but I have a different relationship with touch than most people. I walk arm-in-arm with friends of any gender, I give shoulder rubs to those I know will not misinterpret (which is more people than you might think), I kiss people in public, I hug my friends. I have a rich and full touch life, and it is very important to my well-being.

I have brought these practices into my workshops. After a gradual building of trust within our groups and with full discussion of permissions, boundaries and being true to ourselves, most of our participants absolutely love the touch aspects of our workshops. We teach people how to ask for or to offer something they might like, such as a hand massage, a neck rub or some back pats. We teach them how to use language if they change their minds or if they want to negotiate something other than touch, perhaps a discussion with their partner. We give them a menu of possible touches, areas to stay away from, and then we let them go.

My favorite thing in the world is to watch people as they allow themselves to receive in this way after days, weeks, months or years without this type of non-threatening touch. Just 5 or 6 minutes of deep receiving of someone else's hands can restore the soul.

I know some who read this may be thinking, "I know how to do this. I get massages." I love massage. Massage is a wonderful way

---

[44] J-, W-, L-, D- and J-, thank you a thousand times. And thanks to all of my "alien" friends.

to receive touch, and I endorse it whole-heartedly, with this caveat: when you receive a massage, how much do you truly let go? Do you lay on the table and soak it up, or do you feel obligated to chat with your massage therapist? Do you move your limbs for them instead of letting them move you? Do you truly think about what feels best and ask for exactly that type of touch and at what pressure you find the most pleasurable--throughout the massage, not just at the beginning? Do you ask for more time on your neck or legs or feet if you feel the need, or do you just lay there and hope that your therapist reads your mind?

My massage therapist tells me that I am one of her favorite people to work on because I receive her touch so deeply and completely. She says she is saddened by how many of her clients remain alert throughout the session, moving legs or arms when she would gladly do that for them, or who talk their way through the hour, never really relaxing until the last 10 minutes.

I also am a huge advocate for asking for touch from your loved ones. It's hard to do sometimes. When my partner is very tired and I know it and I'm sitting there with shoulders that feel like a rock, I am often reluctant to ask for some help with that. But, I have found that sometimes I don't just need touch: I need his touch. I need to feel loved and cared for. The receiving of that loving attention for 10 minutes can feel like a 90-minute professional massage in what it does for my mood and my body.

What do we do if we aren't partnered, or if our partner is not interested in touch? There are some options. Many people get pets. Studies have shown that petting a cat lowers the blood pressure, and dogs can make us happier and healthier because they give touch unconditionally, and they generally like to be petted.

If pets are not your thing, you can look into massage, Reiki or other types of hands-on healing. There are workshops that offer optional touch. Another interesting development in touch and touch education is Cuddle Party[45]. The creators of Cuddle Party developed a way to teach people about the importance of touch while offering a safe opportunity to get some great cuddling in. There are cuddle parties in many places in the U.S. now, as well as some other countries.

You can also arrange your own cuddle. Call some friends that you trust and tell them you're having a cuddle or a puppy pile party. Combine it with a video or a discussion if that feels good. It's easy to do, just set up a bunch of blankets or mats on a floor and ask everyone to bring pillows. This may seem like something only teenagers would do but I have 2 friends who are therapists in their 40's who began a group like this, and they love it.

Hugs are another very easy way to increase your touch. You may be surprised how many people are into hugging, if you've never tried it. If it's with someone new, it's a good idea to ask for a hug rather than simply opening your arms for one, because sometimes people will respond to this cue whether they are ready for one or not, trying to be polite. If you ask, you're often likely to get one.

There are a lot of different types of hugs, and you can experiment with which ones feel best to you and your hug partner. I have a dear friend who gives very quick, hard hugs, which was new to me when we first met each other. I have learned that this is what she's comfortable with, and it is now endearing to me. My husband likes long, full body, firm hugs. They are very comforting. I have women friends who give soft, nurturing hugs that are wonderful to receive. Whether it is a quick hug, a long, hug, a soft hug or a firm

---

[45] http://www.cuddleparty.com/

one, all can be great touch experiences and all of them are good for our health and well-being.

The most important part of learning about touch is to learn how to receive it when it is given. When someone touches you, take a deep breath in. Close your eyes. Feel the touch not just on the outside of your skin but also the electricity of it, or the warmth of it, or the flow of it, all the way through into your bones. Keep breathing. Don't respond by touching back. Just receive and feel all of the sensations of that touch. If you can do this for a few minutes, you will either feel rejuvenated and energized, or relaxed and replenished.

If you are with a partner or friend, tell them what you are up to. Let them know that you are practicing receiving. Ask them to give you the touch that feels good to them (and you, of course!), for as long as it feels good to them, and allow yourself to fully accept what they are giving you without giving any touch back. If you truly take in what they are giving, you will naturally fill up and want to touch them back after awhile. Don't rush this. Let it come on its own. Pay attention to what your body needs and wants and enjoy.

Practicing Yes with touch has tremendous and immediate rewards. Our cortisol levels (stress hormones) lower automatically when we receive trusted touch, which is very good for the immune system. Good touch can also lower blood pressure and heart rate. We will feel more relaxed, happier, more supported and more loved.

CHAPTER 13

THE SEX NO

*Y*ou're four years old. You come across an oval object in your parents' room. It's pretty big, you can't fit it in your hands. It's so interesting! It looks like a ball but it's shaped like an egg, and has what look like shoe-laces on the side. And it's such a crazy shape! You throw it on the floor. It bounces, but in all kinds of weird directions. Funny! Soon, you are throw-ing it on the floor over and over again, trying to guess which way it will bounce next. You're having the time of your life.

Suddenly, your Mom walks in. She takes a look at you and her face gets white. "What are you doing?" she asks. You're confused. You stop, knowing something is wrong, but you can't imagine what. "Where did you get that? You're too young for that!" and she grabs it away.

"Mom. Why?" you ask. She doesn't answer. You are completely con-fused. She takes the ball away and you don't see it again for a long time.

A year later, you're in your parents' room again, playing with race-cars while Dad gets ready for work. Your favorite drag racer rolls into the closet. While you're searching the floor, you come across a bunch of material. It is huge, a long piece of fabric with lots of padding. You notice another one like it on the *floor. You pull them out and start playing with them. Dad comes out of the bathroom where he was shaving, and sees the padding spread out on the floor.*

"Whoa, champ!" he laughs, but very nervously. He quickly picks up the pads off the floor and stuffs them into the closet. "Those are not for you, buddy."

"Why? What are they?" you ask.

"Those are for grownups only," he tells you. "Don't touch them, they're OFF LIMITS." He looks at you sternly and you get uncomfortable.

"Yeah, but what ARE they?" you ask again.

Your dad musses your hair, guides you out of the bedroom with his hand on your back. "Never mind, buddy. I'll tell you when you're older."

A few weeks later, you can't sleep. You can hear Mom and Dad downstairs watching TV, so you make your way down the steps. From the stairway you can see that on TV a game is being played. There are men in big huge suits and funny hats running around a green field, and they're throwing that oval thing! It looks really fun, and you start to get really excited watching it. Then, Mom turns around and spies you on the stairs.

She gasps. "John!" she hisses to your Dad. She jumps up and walks quickly toward you, blocking your view. Dad abruptly turns off the TV.

"C'mon, tiger, you're supposed to be in bed," he says, as your mother tries to rush you up the stairs.

This time you won't go. "Yeah, but Dad, what are they DOING???" you insist. Both of your parents look at each other. They look really uncomfortable and nervous. You begin to get nervous, too, and start wishing you hadn't asked.

"It's a game, sport," your father says.

"John!" your mother shoots your Dad a warning look. "Honey, this is one of those things you're too young to understand," Mom says.

"I'm big enough! Tell me about the game," you plead.

"We will, honey, we will. But, this game is really dangerous! People get hurt all the time," Mom explains. "It's not for kids. Now up to bed."

You grumble but you can tell you're not getting anywhere. You can't sleep that night thinking about it. You want to be one of the guys in the big huge suits, throwing that ball around.

Now you're 7. You're over your best friend, Damien's house. You get bored playing war and the two of you sneak into his oldest brother Zach's room. "Look at this!" Damien whispers. He dives into Zach's closet and comes out with an oval ball just like the one you found a long time ago at home.

"My Dad has one of those!" you say excitedly. "What IS it? My parents won't tell me."

"It's called a football," Damien says authoritatively. "It's from a game the grownups play. But, Zach is already into it. He hides his gear in his closet under his old clothes. Mom never looks."

"How do you play?" you ask.

"Well, you start on the yard line."

"What's a yard line?"

"It's a line down the middle of the field. You have to run straight across it, I think. Then, you throw the ball at another guy as hard as you can. And, he throws it back," Damien says proudly.

"What's the point of that?"

"Well, whoever has the ball is the bad guy. Everyone has to beat him up. So, you don't ever want to have the ball for too long, it's bad news."

"Then why would you ever take it?" you ask, perplexed.

"For your teammate, stupid!" Damien says, exasperated. "You can't just always be free. You know, it's like never being the guy who dies when we play war. Everyone has to take turns."

"So how do you win?" you ask.

"I don't know," Damien admits, looking down at the ball in his hands. "I can't get anyone to tell me how it works."

"Throw it to me," you say.

"WHAT? Are you nuts? If Zach finds us here he'll kill me!"

"C'mon! Just throw it," you say.

Damien throws you the ball. You throw it back. It feels really good in your hands. Why is everyone so worried about this? It's fun! Soon, the two of you are throwing the football further and further, laughing. Damien's on Zach's bed, goofing around, tossing the ball down to you, trying to get you to miss it. You're making so much noise you don't hear Damien's mom until she's already in the room.

She looks absolutely shocked. "What....what are you doing?" she whispers. She looks terrible. You try to hide the ball behind your back, but it's too late. "Where did you get that?"

Damien is silent. You say nothing, scared to death.

"Go home," she tells you. "I'll be calling your parents about this."

You walk home, feeling sick to your stomach. Something bad is going to happen now, you know it. When you get home, Mom tells you to go to your room. You wait there for an hour, which feels like forever. Nothing makes you feel better, not your favorite video game, nothing. When Dad gets home you can hear them both talking in hushed tones, arguing about something. You know it has to do with you. Soon, you hear footsteps in the hall.

"Listen, sport, we have to have a talk," Dad begins. Mom is fiddling over and over again with her ring. "We heard about what happened at Damien's today."

You listen, stunned, as your parents tell you that you can't be friends with Damien anymore. He's a bad influence, they say. He's introducing you to things that are for adults and they don't want you to play football anymore. You don't understand. They try to explain that football is dangerous. It's for adults. But, they don't tell you why and by now you've learned not to ask too many questions.

When you're 12, they give you a sports education class at school. Finally, you're going to learn about this from an expert. The teacher is a science teacher. You can't figure out why they put a science teacher in charge of teaching you about football. Your science teacher tells you about the basic rules of football, and the goal. But, he doesn't tell you how you can block a play, how to tackle, when to throw to another player. He spends most of his time talking about how to stay safe, and telling you to wait until you're older to start playing. He shows illustrations of players in uniform, and tells the proper way to put on a uniform. But, he doesn't show you a film of anyone playing, and you've never seen a game, even though you've caught glimpses of it on TV.

When you're fourteen, your Dad sits down with you really awkwardly and gives you the basic rules again, but you learned them a long time ago. You're curious about details, but there's no way you're going to ask him. He tells you that while he understands you might decide to play, he thinks it's better if you wait until you're older, and you are better able to handle it.

Some of your friends' parents give them a five-minute talk with the basic rules, but no details. Some parents give their kids protective gear so if they play they won't get hurt, but those parents are the minority, and gear is expensive.

The older you get, the more you learn about football from other kids and the Internet. Some kids tell you one thing about the way it's played and other kids tell you something else. The Internet has hundreds of stories and websites about how best to play, and what makes the top players so good. But, you've tried it now, and some of the things you read really didn't work. You're not sure who to believe.

You get your own football along the way, and hide it in your closet like everyone else you know. Eventually, there are lots of secret games that go on, on the weekends and places where the parents can't find out. Sometimes, kids get injured, and it's all the gossip at school.

You grow older, and eventually you can play the game whenever you can get enough people, but you've been told over and over again that it's much safer to find a regular team, and play with that team for the rest of your life. That way less people will be hurt. That way you can trust that you are taking the least risks.

But, it's a tough thing. How do you know who you want to spend the rest of your life playing with, when you were never taught how to play the game?

I wrote "Football" a few years ago. I was struck with how much people protested that they were very positive about sex, they just wanted to protect children. But, as I hope the story above depicts, this isn't the whole story. If we were merely worried about children's safety, we would educate them about sex in the same way we do with everything else: by slowly allowing them to explore it--in age-appropriate ways and with appropriate peers. We would teach them to never touch anyone's private parts or bodies without clear permission. We would give them great books to educate them at the right levels[46]. We wouldn't flip out if we found them playing "doctor" or "you show me and I'll show you" with other kids. We would tell them what they needed to know as they grew, including health and prevention information as well as intimacy and relationship skills. We would answer their questions honestly and directly as they got older, and perhaps hand them a copy of The Joy of Sex[47] or some other helpful guide to answer their curiosity as they came into the teen years. We would trust and hope that by talking to them about sex in a positive and holistic way since they were small, they would feel comfortable asking us questions and advice when it was time to make larger decisions such as intercourse, beginning a monogamous relationship, or how to negotiate Internet pornography.

As individuals or parents dealing with children, the fact is that most of the time, no one has taught us a healthy way to deal

---

[46] I love Harris & Emberley's books, It's so Amazing!, It's Not the Stork, and It's Perfectly Normal.

[47] The Joy of Sex, by Alex Comfort This book is still one of the best out there for basic information. For older adolescents (later teens and college-age) I like The Guide to Getting It On, by Goofyfoot Press.

with this subject. Very, very few people that I know in the United States--of any age--were given age appropriate messages and information about sex, and certainly not positive feelings about it.

It hardly needs to be said, some might think, that we have a big NO to sex in our society. Women who have "too much" are seen as sluts. Men who have "too much" are labeled players and people are told to watch out, not to date them. Teenagers are told to abstain. Many children are told not to masturbate[48].

Others would argue the opposite. "Sex is everywhere!" they exclaim. It's on television, on our computers, in movies, in ads. Everything seems to be sold with sex, from breath mints to milk. It is ubiquitous on the Internet. Every type of sexual behavior seems to be available to view from our homes, as long as we have a computer and access to the web. Parents despair of keeping their children away from sexual content.

The fact is, both are true, but not, perhaps, in the way that we think. We are truly polarized in our society, with repressed sexuality on the one hand, and unrestricted commercialism on the other. This last point is extremely important, as *we don't have sexual excess so much as commercial manipulation.* When the two are confused, big problems occur in our psyches.

Let's look at the first point: that sex is repressed today, especially in areas like the U.S., the U.K., Canada and Australia. The subject of my doctoral project was erotophobia, which is the fear of sex, and includes negative attitudes regarding sex. Erotophobia

---

[48] If you yourself are more open and don't believe this, please ask around. I have heard story after story in the past couple of years of people punishing their children for touching themselves, or trying to stop them, even when it happens in private.

is a cultural phenomenon, not just an individual fear. Some might think that such a thing doesn't exist, but if you look closely, you find examples of it everywhere[49].

Nudity erotophobia has caused everything from the banning of *private* nude associations in the United States to many hundreds of women being arrested each year for breast-feeding in public. While it's true that many states now have laws protecting women from this outrageous abuse, it still happens, and it happens because of erotophobia. "It's inappropriate," I have heard on many, many occasions. Yet, disgust always contains fear. And the word "inappropriate" has become a stealthy way to shame someone with a clinical-sounding term.

Homophobia is an aspect of erotophobia that is the root cause of deaths and injuries to thousands of gay, lesbian or transgendered people every year. In 2009, two eleven-year-old boys, one in Massachusetts and one in Georgia took their own lives due to homophobic bullying by their peers. In the end of 2010, we had another rash of young people killing themselves to end their torment. LGBT (lesbian, gay, bisexual, transgender) people are more likely to be treated roughly or poorly by doctors, spurring the building of special health centers for those with alternative orientations. One trans woman, Tyra Hunter, bled to death in an ambulance after EMT's discovered her body was male, and they refused to treat her. Though this is an extreme case, abuse and neglect of LGBT people by homophobic or trans-phobic medical staff is not uncommon.

Fears of sexual variety lead us to create laws where consensual oral sex between partners is illegal in some states. Fear of female

---

[49] For my 3 minute video showing many examples of this, please go to http://instituteforsexuality.com/video-and-materials/ and click on "Sex Scared."

sexuality and of masturbation, make it illegal to sell vibrators in some states. Alabama, Texas and Mississippi have all had anti-sex-toy laws, and although the federal court of appeals ruled the Texas law unconstitutional, Corpus Christi ruled that federal laws were not binding on State courts, keeping the legal ride going round and round, if not merrily. In one brief, the Alabama Attorney General stated: "(the) ban on the sale of sexual devices and related orgasm-stimulating paraphernalia is rationally related to a legiti-mate legislative interest in discouraging interests in autonomous sex."[50] This means that the government of the state of Alabama believes it has a right to tell you what to do--and what NOT to do--in your bedroom, by yourself.

One can hardly fail to notice that this vibrator ban targets fe-male masturbation more than male. Women's sexuality has long been an object of fear and misunderstanding. We don't have to go back to the Bible or to Victorian times, either. When the Kinsey team came out with the book Sexual Behavior in the Human Female in 1953, the uproar that came out of it was largely related to data about female masturbation and orgasm. The public out-rage at this perceived "obscenity" haunted Dr. Kinsey for the rest of his career, despite the fact that investigations by the American Statistical Association found that his research was some of the best ever done on the topic of sexuality.

The Motion Picture Association of America's ratings board is another example of fear of sexuality—especially women's—and sexual pleasure. The suggestion of oral sex given to a man is a fairly common experience in R-rated movies. It is often de-picted in comedy scenes, even in family movies such as the 1989 film "Parenthood" with Steve Martin and Mary Steenburgen. Yet, over and over again the MPAA ratings board has deemed that the

---

[50] Williams v. Prior, October, 2000

suggestion of oral sex given to a woman is so extreme that it deserves an NC-17 rating. One of the most recent was a movie called Charlie Countryman, where just such a scene had to be deleted from the film in order for it to be rated R while the scenes of people's heads being blown off remained uncensored. Killing and torture of all types are perfectly acceptable in any R-rated film. As the late sexology professor Dr. Janice Epp used to say, "Kiss a breast, get an X rating. Shoot a breast, get an R-rating."

Fear of female sexuality is the root cause of much bullying and sexual harassment. Teenage girls and young women are constantly bombarded with warnings about "sexting". While it is true that sending nude pictures of oneself can have some very negative consequences if they are shared with others, this is akin to blaming a rape victim for being sexually assaulted--another problem that is very real and very present, even after many years of activism by women's advocates--but we have yet to make this connection.

The Sex No also dictates who we have sex with: which genders, what ages, what races or ethnicities, even social classes. As far as age, even though we live in the era of "the Cougar", it is still socially difficult for older women to have younger lovers, and men who have significantly younger partners are looked upon as predatory, even if both people are fully adult and clearly in love.

Perhaps on a more common level, the sex No can make us profoundly unaware of, or out of touch with, the feelings in our bodies. This is particularly true of the pelvic region and women's vulvas. It is a sad fact that since becoming a sexologist, I have met many women who have never looked at their vulvas, cannot locate their own clitoris, and cannot orgasm. Some of these women are over 50 years old, and they still do not know the basics about their own bodies. This is not just a pleasure problem, it also causes health issues. Women who are more erotophobic (sex-negative) are also less likely to talk to partners about birth control, less likely to go to the OBGYN and perform fewer Breast Self-Exams (vital for detecting early signs of breast cancer)[51].

So, the sex No is everywhere. Then why, you might ask, do we see sex all over the place, in ads, on television, on the Internet? Doesn't that mean that we have too much sex in this society? The answer is no. We do not have too much sex. We have sexualized commercialism. When we witness a genuine sexual encounter between people, we usually have one of three reactions:

1. Wow, that's hot!
2. Wow, that's beautiful.
3. Yawn, that's boring.

When we witness sexualized commercialism such as half-naked people in ads for jeans, some people feel disgusted. But, if you analyze your reaction, you will find that the disgust is probably not at their nudity. The disgust is because we feel the manipulation of our senses by the ad. We feel the sale, not the sex. We feel that our most vulnerable of emotions (sexual attractiveness, lovability) are being used by the advertising industry, we resent it, and after awhile we confuse sex and manipulation. We get angry that they use sexuality as a tool, so angry that we forget that it isn't real sex we are seeing.

This is true of pornography as well. We really don't know how much porn can influence a person's ideas about what sex is or should be, despite (or maybe because of) the fact that pornography does not depict genuine sexual encounters so much as it sells sexual arousal. If we know that what we're looking at, is in

---

[51] Fisher, Byrne, White & Kelley, 1988

itself a commercial, and that porn is designed to sell more porn (and the commercials associated with it), then perhaps we can enjoy it and/or watch it with few or no negative impacts. But, when we watch it unconsciously, we may also unconsciously begin to think that this is what real sex looks like. We often don't even question it, and many people begin to unconsciously mimic it, without realizing that the poses used to depict sex for the camera are not usually the best positions for real sex. In addition, the activities that we see are often devoid of any true connection between the actors. Men in porn almost never smile or look into their partner's eyes. Women never ask for different positions, or request lube, or say I love you. Everyone always appears to have an orgasm[52].

So, we find ourselves in this society caught between the two realities of fear of sex and sexualized commercialism. How can we find our way back to our genuine sexual response? How can we connect with our true eroticism and pleasure? How can we say a Deep Yes to sex?

---

[52] I have met several porn actors, and the women react with surprise when they are asked if their orgasms on screen are real. Many of them refuse to come on screen, and express that they think that's gross. "That's for my boyfriend," I heard twice. They really are acting, and we shouldn't forget that, even if we enjoy what we see.

CHAPTER 14

THE SEX YES

Fire is not the only element that warms,
But it's the one I can't look away from.
A hundred thousand change, each moment strange
And wild, archaic vision in its many eyes,
The architecture of sorrow and the art of satisfaction in its
breath.
And when it flares I hear
ecstatic,
Inhale creation,
Need nothing.
8/14/09

Sex is the life force. Whether we are trying to reproduce or not, sexual energy comes from the deepest part of ourselves and carries the vitality of our beings. It is truly essential for us to understand that pressure against our natural sexuality causes far more than loneliness, isolated incidents of sadness or fear, or even health concerns. The repression of sex as a whole has the effect of an energetic wet blanket: yes, we still have bodies, but we can't see as well, can't move as well, can't smell as keenly, feel the air or taste our food in the same way. If we want to have whole, healthy lives, we must find our Deep Yes to sex.

Several years ago, I was in a terrible rut in my life. I had a great job, an amazing husband and a loving family but I just felt dead inside. I was listless, depressed and 40 pounds overweight. I had begun to have fantasies about romances or sex with other men. I was searching for something, but I couldn't define what. I had been in therapy many times over the years and found it helpful, but I knew that therapy was no longer the answer.

I found myself considering different ideas. I remember thinking, "Maybe I should practice yoga." "Maybe I should get a massage every week." "Maybe I should try dance and movement therapy." Each of these ideas seemed right on one level, and yet just a little bit off. I was seeking a connection to my body, which was the right track. But, I hadn't found what I needed.

One weekend, I was on a retreat that I have attended every year since my early twenties. One of my favorite parts of this weekend was always the dance on Saturday night. It took place in a large meeting room space with wood-paneled walls and a fireplace at one end, and about 50 of us could dance in there at a time. I found myself dancing with an old friend, a guy I used to have a crush on years before. As I danced, I found my desire for him come back. He was still very handsome and a great dancer. I felt this happen and I began to do what I had taught myself to do for my entire marriage: to shove down the desire, deep into my belly, cut myself off from it by forcibly burying it.

But, suddenly another thought occurred to me. What if I didn't cut it off? What if I let myself have my desire, knowing I didn't have to act on it, just feel it?

The thought was riveting. I kept dancing, and let my desire for this man flow through my body. As I danced, I breathed this energy up from my pelvis and out through my mouth, letting it flow. Suddenly, I was breathtakingly on fire. I felt an enormous amount of energy sweep through my system. The joy and the aliveness that came with it was incredible. The sexual desire for my friend was suddenly a small thing. Instead, I felt The Desire coursing through me. I felt as though all the desire I had ever had ran through my system, and instead of feeling it as a longing or a lack, it felt like the greatest empowerment I had ever known. Empowered desire. My entire being was a focused flame.

The energy that came with this experience was intense. I felt as though I might die with the passion of it. It flowed out of me, into the room, and out into the night beyond. It took a lot of self-talk and channeling to refrain from seeking an outlet for it with another person. Instead, I put it into the dance. I couldn't sleep that night. I lost sleep for many other nights afterward, but it felt wonderful. I was plugged in to a power source that had no limit.

It took me two or three years to realize that I had unknowingly awakened what is often called Kundalini Shakti, the life force, that night. My intention to feel my feelings fully, the dancing and the breath work had all enabled it. The next few months were difficult, but worth every moment. I went to Weight Watchers and over the next year lost 40 pounds, leaving me at a healthy weight. My husband was in a depressed time in his life and in chronic tension, and I was obsessed with different men. I confided in friends about my obsessions, went back to my therapist, wrote pages and pages in my journals, and cried a lot.

I did not cheat on my husband, and I thank God for that to this day, not only because it would have damaged my marriage but because by channeling the energy into my self-discovery, I opened up something much larger than a sexual or love affair. I found the courage to confront these long-standing issues with him. We both remember the conversation to this day, standing in our kitchen together, terrified and unsure what to do. Our sexual connection had been damaged by years of fertility problems. He recognized that he had been depressed and had little energy for anything but his work. The tension he was under had been causing him chronic pain in his back and legs, making lovemaking an occasional and often lukewarm experience. I told him I had been obsessing about other men and that something in our sex life had to change.

Together, we came up with a plan. We had a friend who taught erotic spirituality workshops, and we called him. He recommended a retreat in northern California, and we registered. On the way up there, we laughed and joked nervously about the upcoming event. We were afraid, but excited, as well.

At the retreat, we were introduced to some principles of Tantra, an ancient Indian practice that includes breath work, meditation, and awareness of energy in the body[53]. This experience opened us up in ways that have reverberated into every area of our lives. It helped us to re-connect with each other sexually, and to find some great ways to reignite our relationship. After a second retreat that year, my husband began breathing and meditation practices. His chronic back and leg pain disappeared, and has not come back. It has been nine years since then. He is a new man, full of vitality and humor.

---

[53] If you are reading this and it sounds good to you, please be careful seeking it for yourself. Our Tantra teacher was taught by an Indian scholar and Tantra master. Poorly trained Tantra teachers can actually be damaging to their students.

As for me, my entire energy shifted. Work took new turns. I got a job as a radio personality four nights a week on a show that talked about sex and relationships. When the show was canceled after a year and a half, I was already back in school. I had always wanted a doctoral degree so that I could study something very deeply but I had decided I wasn't going to go until I knew exactly what I wanted to study. I now had my answer...it was human sexuality. In all of the years of taking care of myself--therapy, 12-step meetings, Weight Watchers, exercise, quitting smoking--I had found this glaring missing piece of the wellness puzzle.

I have asked myself often why sex should be such an important area to say Yes to. Would learning about our sexual energy be as important if we lived somewhere where it wasn't so repressed? My answer at the moment is that it would. The repression, trivialization and vilification of sex in our society makes our energy much flatter and our circumstances more dire, it is true, but since sex is the embodiment of the life force, then understanding how to keep this energy flowing and alive is essential in any culture.

In order to understand how broad the importance of erotic energy is in your own body, you have only to remember a time when you felt newly in love. When we fall in love, our erotic being opens up to the world. Suddenly, colors seem brighter. Food tastes better or becomes less important because we feel so good we can barely eat. We want to stay up all night composing poetry to him, or talking with them on the phone for hours. We have a spring in our step, we have a twinkle in our eye that no one can miss...in short, we feel fantastic. Some scientists will point to hormones or neurotransmitters that cause this phenomenon, but most of us are not that cynical. We know that love caused the chemistry in our bodies to change, not the other way around.

Most people know this feeling, this wonderful, amazing, chaotic feeling of being in love. This is what we feel like when our erotic selves are wide open. But, what if you were told that we were meant to live in a similar state most of the time, with no particular lover to focus on and distract us from our daily duties, but instead just a sense of overall well-being and connectedness to the world? What if you understood that this was not only possible, not only desirable, but also imperative for your health and happiness, and the good of the world?

The truth is that the sex No cuts us off from our lower bodies, sometimes almost entirely. In energetic terms, it represses the first and second energy centers (chakras) in the lower parts of our body. The sex No interferes with the flow of power from the very source of our energy at the base of our spines. In India this source is called *Shakti* or *Kundalini*, and there are entire yoga practices set up to awaken it and channel this energy[54]. In fact, the word Shakti comes from the Sanskrit *shak*, meaning "to be able".[55] All power, to do anything, create anything, manifest anything, rests in Shakti.

If this language doesn't work for you, that's OK. We don't have to tap into Indian tradition to understand that sex power is the power of creation. It is the energy that creates new life. In fact, it IS life. Early sexologists knew this, calling the life drive "libido", and linking it to the desire for sexual connection.

Now, imagine what happens when we ignore, neglect, vilify or trivialize the lower half of our bodies because we have been taught

---

[54] Please do not seek to awaken kundalini energy without a very experienced, very wise teacher with deep background in yoga or *eastern* tantra. This energy can be very volatile if pushed or forced.
[55] Shakti is also seen as a Goddess, the embodiment of feminine energy and power.

that sex is wrong, immoral, inappropriate, self-indulgent, juvenile, trivial, or even evil. I'm not suggesting that we abandon everything and go wild (though for some people, this has been one path to enlightenment and freedom). I'm suggesting that if we create a big NO around sex, we create a big NO around our power because we confuse sexuality and eroticism. We must learn how to love our sexuality rather than be afraid of it. We must learn how to open up the lower parts of our bodies' energies so that we can manifest change when we need to, bring new energy into our lives when we want to, and connect with others in a much more loving and open way. We cannot do this if we are too afraid of sex because we will encounter sexual energy when we open up these centers; sometimes a LOT of sexual energy, and this can be frightening if we don't know what to do with it.

Beginning Yes Practices for Sex

Of all of the Yeses that I have written about in this book, the sex Yes is one of the most difficult for people to let themselves have. I'm not saying that most of us don't manage to have sex, and even satisfying or good sex. But, most of us have shut down our bodies to such an extent that we don't realize how numb we are at all. We have no idea that sex can be a highly ecstatic experience, and if we do know that, the vulnerability that comes with that thought often terrifies us.

We can begin by ourselves. On a piece of paper or in a journal, explore some questions for yourself. Some of them might include your parent's attitudes toward sex, how you learned about it, what kind of formal sex education you had, and what your first sexual experiences were like. (If your first sexual experiences were involuntary, it's very important to focus on the voluntary ones, as well).

You also want to explore what messages have you received about sex as you got older, and where your sex life is right now (alone and/or with a partner or partners).

Who do you talk to about sex? Do you have friends you can discuss anything with? Is sex an acceptable topic for you and those close to you? If you have a problem, who would you go to? If things are good, who can you tell who would be happy for you and welcome to hear it?

Once you have written these things down, you can begin to have a more comprehensive understanding of the messages that you received about sex, the attitudes you may have around sex, and the things that may block you from having better sex. This, in turn, leads us toward embracing sex as a Deep Yes for ourselves.

Exploring the Sex Yes With Yourself

This topic scares the daylights out of a lot more people than you may imagine. I'm not talking just about masturbation, though that is very important. I'm talking about getting in touch with your sexual self in a mindful, conscious and thoughtful way. Many people look at sex like going to the bathroom, or taking a shower. It's just something that the body needs, they think. Not much effort is put into it.

Sexual self-pleasure is one of the most powerful practices of The Deep Yes, because its primary purpose is to make you feel good. You're not trying to reproduce, you're not trying to please someone else, you're not trying to impress, you're not trying to gain something from someone else. Masturbation is about YOU, and your pleasure. Fantasy is about YOU, and your pleasure. Saying Yes to your sexuality is an inside job, requiring no one else. How can you deeply receive yourself as a sexual human being?

Questions for Yourself Now

- What are your attitudes *right now* toward your sexual pleasure?
- Do you believe that sex is really good for you--healthy, spiritual, playful, hot?
- Do you get it that you really deserve to feel as good as you want to?
- What is your attitude toward ecstasy?
- What would happen if you decided to explore the depths and heights of ecstasy? Does it scare you to think about that? Does it excite you?
- What would happen if you got everything that you always wanted in terms of pleasure?

These questions are important ones to ask ourselves, especially the last one, because many of us actually have an unconscious belief that if we have too much pleasure, we will die. This may seem ridiculous at first, but if you think about it, it is not. If you've seen the movie Like Water for Chocolate you know that there is just such a scene where ultimate fulfillment ends in the ultimate tragedy. This is a deep-seated belief that many of us are not even aware that we have. We have sayings that reinforce this:

"All good things must end." (So must all bad things, but no one says this.)

"That's too good to be true." (No one says that's too bad to be true.)

Some feel that ecstasy must be paid for with pain and punishment. Others think that if we feel true ecstasy, our lives will be instantly fulfilled and therefore must end. It is also possible that death is the ultimate ecstasy, and we therefore make unconscious comparisons between ecstasy and death. In fact, the French call orgasm "La petite mort"—the little death.

The good news is, we don't die from deep fulfillment of ecstasy. In fact, we can use it to further our growth, to pour excess joy onto others, to get closer to God or the Divine, to have fun, to gain greater health, to be creative. Using sex as a way to access ecstasy is great because we don't need others to do so, we don't need a priest or a temple, and we don't need money.

If you have never masturbated, it's never too late to learn. There are wonderful books for women such as Betty Dodson's classic "Sex for One",[56] and Lonnie Barbach's "For Yourself".[57] For men and male-identified people, I recommend a website, http://orgasmicyoga.com. It is a great website for any gender or orientation, actually, but I particularly like it for men because the type of masturbation practice on there is rarely seen or practiced. It is conscious and sensual, and can connect a man or male-identified person more deeply with his body. If you are very new to these ideas, it may take some getting used to, but take some time and keep an open mind, the payoff is beyond what you can imagine.

Two Words: SLOW DOWN

Many people take only a few minutes to masturbate, and they act as though it's just a bodily function like going to the bathroom that they have to get over with quickly. But, a Deep Yes self-pleasure practice can include long, slow explorations where we take our time with ourselves to truly enjoy. What does it mean to enjoy?

---

[56] http://dodsonandross.com
[57] For Yourself, by Lonnie Barbach

En = inside, to take in. So, when we enjoy, we are internalizing joy. We are bringing joy into our bodies, our psyches, our spirits. YES!

Although many people do not know this, the mechanisms for orgasm and ejaculation are actually separate from each other. Men can learn to detect the difference in their bodies at specific points in their arousal and can have orgasms without ejaculation, making multiple orgasms possible. Masturbation is the best way to begin practicing these skills for those who are interested in trying it out[58].

Whatever you try with these practices, make sure to practice Yes all the way through the process. This means that after you finish, whether you have had an orgasm or not, be still for several minutes afterward and just let yourself experience whatever is happening in your body. The after-effects of sexual activity are as important as the sex itself. If you fall asleep right afterward, or jump up and shower, you can miss incredible sensations of peace, relaxation, fulfillment, closeness, happiness and gratitude. I cannot emphasize the importance of this step enough, so I'm going to repeat it: after you practice some self-pleasuring or have an orgasm, SIT WITH IT. Listen to your body. Experience what is happening in the afterglow. *Deeply receive* what you have given yourself.

It is a Tantric principle that everything is an experiment[59]. Try one or two of these ideas above for a set period of time (2 weeks to 1 month is usually good), and pay close attention to what happens. What happened at first? Did this change over time? What have you noticed in your body? Your energy? Your mood? Your life overall? Your health? Your pleasure? It's not enough to do something new.

---

[58] You can also look at Mantak Chia's book, The Multi-Orgasmic Man

[59] From Kali Rising, Rudolph Ballantine

Paying close mind to the results is an imperative part of our process. A journal can be an invaluable tool for these experiments.

Once you find something that seems to gift you with a new experience or an expansion of yourself, you can practice this one thing over and over again to see what it does for you, or you can try something else. Enjoy the process, and know that it is one of the best things you can do for yourself.

Exploring the Sex Yes With Others

Some who are reading this now are feeling some trepidation. This makes sense to me. I don't want people to be afraid of sex, but I am aware that sex is the one practice on this planet that can both create life and take it away. As such, it has tremendous power, and I think we are right to have respect for it, no matter whether we are currently using it for recreation, procreation, personal growth, fun, spiritual connection, exercise, stress relief or deeper intimacy.

Sex can require tremendous vulnerability; physically, emotionally and spiritually. This is true for all genders. How can we begin to explore receiving in this area?

I am often saddened by how much my college students are focused on sexual performance. Males are often concerned with size and staying power. Females are often concerned with their pleasuring techniques and their body images. Transgender folks are often concerned with feeling congruence between who they know themselves to be and what their bodies' realities are. It's become rare to find a person who simply allows themselves to explore what is pleasurable with another person, and gracefully receives the pleasure offered from that person. Sex has become all about what to do rather than how to be with each other. It can become a contest of who made who feel what, or who did what to whom rather than a deeply pleasurable experience of the body.

Deep receiving sexually is an ecstatic experience. The surrender to the pleasure of someone else's hands can be the most relaxing and most joyful happening in our lives, if we allow it. Do we say yes to being pleasured? Do we allow someone to use their lips, tongues, hands, fingers, toes on us to bring us to ecstasy? Do we allow someone to facilitate our orgasm, or are we afraid to let go that deeply? Do we let our partners play with us, allow them to explore our bodies, or do we get worried that they will be bored, or that we are being selfish? Can we let go of control long enough to be deeply satisfied?

The best lovers I have ever had, have been those who let me please them, as well as pleasing me, and from whom I can see the most true response. There's something about witnessing someone surrendering to that enjoyment that is the hottest thing in the world. When you drive someone to the 10th degree of bliss, where they can barely contain themselves, you get incredible pleasure of your own. This is not just a control freak thing, as some cynically assume. It is true excitement, and it is stunningly beautiful. So, the question is, are you allowing your lover or lovers to have the full pleasure of witnessing yours, or are you curtailing your own and your lover's pleasure by prohibiting or putting caps on how much they are allowed to please you?

How can we begin to say a Deep Yes to sex? How can we practice true receiving in the bedroom--or against that tree, or on that rug in the living room, or on the bathroom sink?

We can start by assuming that sex is a good thing, that it is healthy and wonderful and brings us joy. We can be conscious that happiness is good for us, and use this mantra: "Pleasure is healing"[60]. Some of us will start here, and use these ideas to open ourselves more fully. Some will dive right into the sexual arena and realize these ideas through experiences of the body. Either way is great.

We can seek out new sexual experiences by slowing sex down rather than speeding it up. Most sexual self-improvement books or articles are about expanding our sexual repertoire through toys, role playing, or dress up. These things are terrific ideas, but we can start much more simply if we like, merely by being very mindful and very curious while being sexual with someone else. Treat everything like an experiment, and assume nothing. Assume nothing about what is pleasurable, or not. Assume nothing about the presence or absence of orgasm. Assume nothing about any kind of order that things must have. Take all judgments about what is right or wrong out of the picture except mutual consent. Take all goals out of the picture and play. Rest afterward, and deeply take in the sensations and information. Allow. Receive.

Later, gather the data. What happened? What did you enjoy? What was not so pleasurable? What did your partner enjoy? Did you surprise yourself? Did your partner surprise you? Did you allow yourself to deeply receive? Did you enjoy your partners' pleasure? Which were the most intense experiences for you? Which were the most blissful? The most relaxing? The most boring? The most exciting? The most physically stimulating? All of these experiences are separate pieces of the dance of sex, and all offer different flavors for the feast.

There are so many ways to enjoy sex with a partner that there are libraries worth of books on the topic. It is a vast arena. Exploring

---

[60] Rudolph Ballantine, Kali Rising

sex can mean multiple partners or one partner. It can mean multiple genders or one gender. It can mean multiple new behaviors or going more slowly and consciously with the old ones. We can spend our entire lives exploring sex, and we will never exhaust the possibilities. I won't go into too much here. I will say 2 things that I consider vital:

1. Consensual behavior is the standard for healthy behavior that will add to your happiness and that of your partner/s. This is true whether you're using handcuffs and a flogger or whether you're exploring new ways to kiss.
2. Listen, listen, listen to your body. Even if you just did something that would have shocked you a month ago, your body, not your mind, will tell you truthfully whether or not it's good for you. The body doesn't lie. Do you feel sated, relaxed, replete? Do you feel a deep sense of satisfaction in your belly or lower abdomen? Do you feel closer to your partner/s and more trusting of them? Then, it was probably good for you. Do you feel sad, upset, a bad feeling in your chest, further away from your partner/s? Then there are 2 possibilities: 1) the behavior was OK (consensual, enjoyable, satisfying), but you are still judging yourself for it or 2) the behavior is simply not for you. Even if you intellectually can find no problem with the behavior, if you were not satisfied and enjoying yourself while doing it, don't ignore this sign.

A student of mine sometimes found fantasizing about rape very exciting, and she had two ways to fantasize about it. In one fantasy, the woman ended up enjoying the sex, even though she had not chosen it. In the second fantasy, she was the man who forced a woman who truly did not want him. She found the second fantasy wildly exciting, but when she had an orgasm from it, she always felt a terrible, heavy feeling in her chest and her heart while she came, and it did not go away for several minutes afterward.

She told herself that it shouldn't matter what she fantasized about, since there were no real people involved, but her body told her differently. She doesn't use the second fantasy anymore, and has found others to replace it.

If we listen to our bodies, determine the Yes from ourselves and from others, and deeply receive the pleasure that is being offered to us or that we are offering ourselves, we will change our whole lives.

The Intellectual Exploration of Sex

When we begin to explore our sexual attitudes, needs, hopes and fears, it is good to do it with others. It's extremely helpful to talk about it with other people, to learn how vast the variety is in human sexual behavior, and to realize that we are not alone. Why? Because we receive sexualized commercial messages every day, and we must have some way to counter this onslaught—to unlearn the ideas that sex is a commodity to be bartered with, that sex is about beauty or glamour, that sex is for the young, or that sex is power.

In the 1960's a process called Sexual Attitude Re-Structuring (SAR) was created by the National Sex Forum. The National Sex Forum was originally a group of clergy and people from religious organizations who were attempting to understand what was happening with the sexual revolution in the culture at the time. As a result of their own research, many of them became enlightened and open-minded sexuality educators who developed the SAR in order to help people to take a look at their own attitudes about sexuality, and the impact of these attitudes on people's lives.

Since then, many people have adapted this process (now often called Sexual Attitude Reassessment), and there are now workshops all over the United States that use this process to help examine and reduce the fears and stigmas that we have inside of ourselves about various aspects of human sexuality. To find a good quality SAR class, visit aasect.org online and look under Education, then "Continuing Education". These SAR workshops have been approved by the American Association of Sex Educators, Counselors and Therapists.

We can also create community for ourselves in this process of discovery. Meetup.com is a great website that allows people to find others with particular interests to meet in person. They have everything from quilting groups to sexuality discussions to entrepreneurs. Three of my colleagues and I have recently founded a discussion group in CT for this purpose. If you're motivated to start you can create your own meetup, suited to your needs at this time.

Another way to begin, is simply to start talking to friends or a group you're already part of. Anyone you like who is similarly intrigued by the topic can join your new discussion group. Some women find that they only want to discuss sex with other women. Some LGBT folks feel similarly. Don't feel guilty if you want to limit the group or make it by invitation-only. Feeling safe to discuss sex is a must.

People with particular sexual interests are lucky, because we are living in an age when most anything that we might be interested in can be found on the Internet. I'm not just talking about watching videos[61] or meeting partners, I mean that if you are serious about exploring and understanding yourself, you can find community forums and discussion boards on almost any sexual activity. This is a good place to begin if you have never tried something and want

---

[61] I usually don't recommend watching most porn in order to understand how to have good sex, because it is created for commercial purposes and often does not depict techniques that are the most deeply pleasurable to most people. Porn can, however, be fantasy material for many people.

to know more about it, but keep in mind that people on discussion boards are not necessarily experts, and not all of them will be honest.

If you are looking for ways to give a partner pleasure, or would like some resources for new ways for your partner to touch you, The New School of Erotic Touch[62] has some wonderful videos that demonstrate erotic massage including various types of genital massage. I love these videos because they demonstrate Deep Yes experiences. The massages take time, are involved, and help a person build up to a greater ecstasy by stimulating multiple areas of each organ.

To sum up the discussion about the Deep Yes to sex: it is right and good to allow sex to be an important thing in your life. It is enriching to understand, embrace and receive your own pleasure, which is healing. It is normal and healthy to want a good sexual connection with partners, connections that grow better with time. If we begin to say Yes to sex, we will find that many other creative ventures and transformations begin to take place as well.

---

[62] http://www.eroticmassage.com/

CHAPTER 15

THE LOVE YES

Who would give a law to lovers? Love is unto itself a higher law.

~BOETHIUS, *THE CONSOLATION OF PHILOSOPHY*, A.D. 524

Who, being loved, is poor?

~OSCAR WILDE

This whole book has been about saying Yes to love--loving our bodies, loving our minds, loving our souls. It is about receiving love in our food, in our sleep, in our touch. Yet, one of the more difficult things for people in Western cultures seems to be how to receive love from others. We often don't recognize it when it is in front of us. Even when it is obvious, we often swat it away. We only allow ourselves to receive from tiny groups of people: certain family members, spouses or partners, good friends—and we're often not very good at receiving love from them, either.

After my own big healing, I observed myself noticing things that I had never noticed before as acts of love. Impersonal, sometimes, and yet still acts of love. I was standing in an elevator one morning and I saw the weight limit posted on the wall. It suddenly occurred to me that there are tens of thousands of engineers in the world who work together to create mechanisms and systems to make our lives easier, and to keep us safe. I could have seen the weight-limit sign in a cynical way: as a protection from liability. Though this may be true, it's not accurate or fair to the human race to focus on merely that and ignore the other side of the story—that many people worked for years to help advance our technology so that we would be safe. Plenty of those people cared more about the riders in the elevators than the possible liabilities should there be failure. And I saw the hope and beauty in this every day, ordinary thing.

I began to notice when people opened doors for me or for others. We can call this common courtesy, but the fact is, it's a small piece of love. It's a matter of concern for the well-being of others, and it's often delivered with a smile. To receive it, I have only to say "thank you" and go first, rather than insisting, "Oh, no, after you!" I don't have to do this every time, it's fine for me to open the door, too, but I should do it often, and consciously, and allow myself to receive this gift.

I also did something else. I bought a greeting card with a beautiful photo of an open rose on the front. My name, Rosalyn, means "beautiful rose", so I decided to use the rose as a symbol for myself. I taped it next to my bed so that each morning it was one of the first images that I saw. When I awoke, I looked at the photo and imagined the open rose in my chest, as if it were my heart. I practiced picturing my heart as a full-blown rose throughout the day, and it transformed me. I became more open, happier, and I saw love everywhere.

I see smiles, when I am in a Deep Yes mode. Smiles are another small part of love. In New England, a smile to a stranger is rarer than in other parts of the country. We don't avoid your eye because we want to be rude, we avoid because we want to be polite. We assume that you'd rather go about your business than stop and talk. It's a strange cultural thing, but as a native, I understand it. Yet smiles are more powerful in New England exactly *because* they are rarer here. If I see a smile, I smile myself, and the next thing I know a whole street is smiling.

I noticed this yesterday in a Japanese restaurant near me. A family was at the Hibachi table with their little boy. He was probably 4. The chef came out, cracking jokes and doing a show with his big knives and some eggs. The little boy's delight was creating smiles in all of the servers, and I realized that I hadn't even been noticing that, or taking it in. I began to watch more carefully, pay more attention, focus on the laughter, the wide grin on the boy's face, the way the servers responded, and the happiness that his response gave the Hibachi chef. In seconds, I felt great. I was smiling, happy, laughing. Everyone in that restaurant was loving that little boy that afternoon, and I said Yes to being part of it.

I have learned, too, how to ask for what I need or want. I didn't know how to do this when I was younger. To ask for some touch, or a hug, or a listening ear was beyond my emotional education. But, as I learned that it was OK to need, I learned it was OK to ask for what I needed or wanted, and I became much less worried that I would be turned down, because as I learned to take in, I had more and more people in my life. If one friend said no to a talk, a neck rub, or a ride somewhere, another often said yes.

It's amazing how these cycles will go: If I am afraid to be vulnerable, I am afraid to need. If I am afraid to need, I have fewer people in my life because people remind me that I need. The fewer people I have in my life, the more that I have to rely on a tiny subset of folks to give me what I need. The more that I rely on a tiny group, the more stress is on that group to provide what I need, and I sense this, so I don't ask very often. If I don't ask very often, I hardly ever get what I need. If I hardly ever get what I need, I feel lonely and more vulnerable, and I have less to give to others. So the cycle continues.

There is another cycle that brings me out of this mess. I allow myself to be vulnerable and to receive love, knowing it is what I need. Because I allow vulnerability, I allow more people in my life. Because I have more people, there are more people to fulfill my needs. Because there are more people to fill my needs, I feel less afraid to ask for what I need, knowing it is less of a burden on each of them. The more that I ask for what I need and get it, the less fearful I become and the easier it is to ask for what I need. The more times I ask and my needs are filled, the happier I am as a person, and the more I have to give to others.

There are little ways to say Yes. My husband will say he's going to do the dishes after a meal, and there are many times when I just do them anyway. Why don't I say Yes to his offer? I tell myself that it's because I want the dishes done a certain way, but this isn't really true. It's more true that I am stuck in a No mode, stuck in performance mode, and I don't want to relax because I'm avoiding something. Saying Yes to his dishwashing allows me the opportunity to appreciate his contributions, to talk to him about my day, to listen to him crack jokes. It's also a gift to him, because he likes to give to me.

When you begin to consciously receive what is around you, the whole world suddenly feels different. You can sense a subtle and powerful web of care, concern, attention and holds the world that runs like a beautiful, sparkling hammock. Interconnectedness becomes apparent.

I sometimes use an exercise I call "Who Made Your Breakfast?" with my students to demonstrate how interdependent we are on each other. The concept is simple. I ask people who ate breakfast that morning to raise their hands. I choose one student and I ask, "Who made your breakfast?" They usually say, "I did." I ask, "Are you sure?" They nod and then I'll ask them what they had. A bowl of cereal with milk is a common answer. Well, who made the cereal? Eyebrows go up. Kellogg's, a student might quip. The class laughs. I push it further. Who planted and sowed the oats? Who dried the oats? Who planted and harvested the sugar cane? Who dried the sugar into crystals? Who brought the sugar to the warehouse? Who built the machines that harvested the sugar and the oats? Who mined the metal for the machines? Who made the trucks that bring the cereal to markets? Who drilled the oil for the gas for those trucks? Who refined that oil? Who felled the trees to make the cardboard to make the box to contain the cereal? At this point, the class is often laughing. Millions of people made your cereal, I inform them. And we haven't even gotten to your milk or your coffee!

Understanding interdependence is a great gift in the practice of the Deep Yes. Americans like to think of themselves as independent, and they see the only other option as dependence. But the truth of our existence is interdependence, in so many ways. This truth is wonderful because once we realize that we need everyone and everything, we suddenly realize that this means the world needs us, too. We are never unnecessary, trivial or unimportant. There are ways that the world and other people need us that we will never even discern. It also keeps us from becoming too fear-driven in our egos. We are not the Be-All-And-End-All for our children, our spouses or partners, or our employers. What a relief! We can relax and be less perfectionistic, less anxiety driven, and we can allow others to help with kids, parental care, or projects at work.

The Yes of Relationship & Romance

Our partners can be the hardest people to say yes to. It seems it would be the opposite, and in the beginning of a love affair, this is often true. We allow our lovers into space in our hearts that we never imagined anyone could enter. We revel in our surrender, our vulnerability. It seems nothing feels better than this Yes.

As time goes on, though, sometimes that very vulnerability that we had in the beginning can become subtly--often unconsciously--disturbing or threatening. The more that we know someone, commit our lives to someone, the more vulnerability we have with them. When the rush of new love energy wears off, we aren't quite as love-drugged as we were. Then we often back up, we don't surrender quite as deeply, we don't receive quite as easily in the bedroom, with our love-talk, or even with the dishes.

I have a file on my phone, and one on my computer, called "Reminders: D". This file consists completely of wonderful things that my husband has said to me about how he feels about me. I keep this list for a few reasons. The first is because I won't remember the exact words, and he often says lovely, poetic things that I want to remember in detail. "I love you" is wonderful but it feels different than "you are the love of my life", or "you bring me so much joy". Second, I don't fully take in what he says to me a good portion of the time. I hear the words but they don't settle in, they don't reverberate in my system the way that they did when we first met. Sometimes, I need to look at them later to truly appreciate what he said, and writing them down helps me to do this. Thirdly,

I can get into telling myself stories about him that are not true when I'm angry, frustrated or stressed out. I tell myself he doesn't care about me, or that he isn't thinking about me, and it makes me unhappy. When I re-read these reminders, they keep me in reality: he loves me, he appreciates me, he wants me and he likes me.

Resistance to Relationship as a No

I have often heard single straight women complain, "There are no quality men out there". I hear this from all ages of women. Young women say that young men are afraid of commitment, and older women say there are no quality single/divorced men because they're all married. I hear single gay men complain about men with commitment issues, that a guy who wants a good settled relation-ship is impossible to find, and I have heard single lesbians say that the pool of women for them is tiny, so it must be this that makes finding a good relationship so hard. Bisexual/pansexual folks bemoan their plights, saying that no one will date them because straight people think they will leave them for a gay person, and gay people think they will leave them for a straight one. Straight single guys complain that, "All women are crazy".

There may be some truth to some of these claims at different points in our lives. Yet, sometimes we blame our circumstances for our own lack of openness to a new situation. I was at a work-shop one time and watched a very dramatic example of just how blind we can make ourselves when we don't want to see. A woman in my small group was saying that she couldn't find a good man who wanted her, and spent time talking about how hard it was. A good-looking man of her age in the group responded genuinely, saying that he found her very attractive and he would love to go out with her. This man was a successful professional, he was very attractive, he was funny, and he was a good communicator, as he had demonstrated all week. After a very slight pause, she went on talking about her situation as if he had not spoken. She simply did not want to let go of her story that there was no one available for her. She was not ready to look at her own fears of vulnerability.

It is one thing to exercise choice, and to know that we want chemistry, as well as other types of connection. But, sometimes attraction and chemistry are influenced by our own internal yeses and nos. Was this woman's "no" there because she wasn't attracted to him, or because she couldn't imagine a Yes for herself? Despite her spoken desire for a partner, she didn't respond with a Yes to anyone who expressed interest that weekend.

Many people are afraid to date multiple people, and yet this is exactly what we need to get through this idea that "there is no one out there". When I got serious about settling down, I decided to join a dating service (this was before internet dating). I had a hunch that I probably would not find the love of my life at a dating service, and I didn't. But, I figured that dating would remind me that there are many single people, all searching like I was, and would give me something to do and some company, if nothing else. It was a change from waiting for Mr. Perfect to show up in my life somewhere. It worked. Although I never met someone I could really click with, I always had something to do, someone to go places with, I met some really great people and I had some fun. This, in turn, made me more attractive to others because I was busy and happy, and it made me more hopeful and allowed me to focus on positive things going on in my life. As Robin Williams has quipped, if you can't have Mr. Right, there is at least Mr. Right Now.

As far as Mr. Right, I wouldn't be with my husband if I hadn't given up my Relationship No paradigm. I had known him and been attracted to him for quite awhile. We were both part of the same training consortium, and one summer the organizers had a workshop for us at someone's home. I was excited he was there, and tried to sit near him when I could. I knew little about him, and I was having fun learning more about who he was. At lunch time, I was sitting next to him having a great time when someone mentioned having a hard time waking up, and he talked about how he and his girlfriend had different alarm clock times, making it difficult for him that summer.

I was crushed. I wanted to leave the table to go to the bathroom and cry. Here we go again, I thought. Another great guy, and I get so excited about him, and he's unavailable. What the hell? Why does this always happen to me? –and on and on. In the midst of it, though, I stopped myself. I had been working on being positive, on thinking differently, and on being more open. It occurred to me that he hadn't said that the girlfriend was a current one. Maybe she was an ex. I had assumed the worst. I forced myself to consider that there were more possibilities than one. For some reason, this perspective was profound. My exact thoughts were, "It may be, and it may not be, but it's *possible*. It's a possibility." This will sound dramatic, but I felt everything around me shift. It was as if I entered an alternate reality.

I got up from the table and poured myself some coffee. He was in the kitchen talking to someone who was congratulating him on buying a house recently. This could have been another reason to think he was in a committed relationship, but I struck up a conversation and asked him about the house. I followed it up by asking if he had bought it with someone and if he was he getting married? To which he replied, "No, in fact, I just broke up with someone. I bought it myself."

This was the beginning of the rest of my day, which was stellar. We were put into small groups to role-play training scenarios, and he was in mine. I later found out he arranged to switch groups so that he could be with me. By the end of the day, I was pretty sure he was interested in me, and of course he was. Although this is a fun story about us getting together, it is also an extremely important one in my personal growth. My negativity could have killed this relationship in the bud. Instead, I opened up my paradigm to include infinite possibilities, and I felt the whole world change.

Saying Yes to Our Partners' Love

When we have been partnered or married with someone for awhile, it can often become harder rather than easier to say Yes to them. We forget that they love us. We forget that we love them. We become focused on day-to-day difficulties instead of day-to-day joys. How can we say Yes to our partners' love?

We can start with noticing what they do for us. Little things are fine: laundry, dishes, riding the kids somewhere. It doesn't matter if they are "our laundry" and "our kids" or that "He *should* take them to baseball, they belong to both of us anyway", instead let's focus on the fact that they do these things. Take the "should" out of it and just appreciate, and *receive*, what is. What did your partner do for you today, no matter how small? Did they tell you they love you, put dishes in the dishwasher, go to work for the family, make love with you? How well did you receive it? Can you spend a second or two taking a deep breath and taking it in?

When your partner touches you, do you pay attention? Do you take in the kiss on the cheek, the hug, the brush on the arm? If she grabs you from behind, can you stop what you're doing long enough to receive it, say Yes to it, hug her arms closer to you and feel it? If they nuzzle your neck can you lean into it, feel the pleasure of it, flirt?

Think of some small, daily ways that you can receive what your partner gives you. Notice. Breathe them in. Then, thank them for what they do. Research has shown that expressing thanks or gratitude actually makes us happier, not just the person hearing our thanks[63].

Gender Differences, Closeness, and Accepting Sex as Love

Deborah Tannen's research[64] shows that men often want to have sex in order to feel close, but women often want to feel close in order to have sex. This can be true of any gender, actually, though it seems to style in these broad directions. Ask yourself, no matter your gender, do I prefer to feel close to someone before I have sex? Or do I often want to have sex in order to feel closer to my partner? If you are partnered or married, ask them the same question.

This is incredibly important, because people who want to feel close prior to having sex can feel that their partner is insensitive if he or she wants to have sex when there has been little connection. The standard way this is expressed is, "All he wants is sex." In this statement, there is a lack of understanding that many people connect *through* sex, it is their way of feeling closer, they feel more intimate by sharing this together, and it is an avenue for these things rather than a desire for physical pleasure alone.

If you have a partner who connects through sex, it's important to know, especially if you trend in the other direction. When they ask you for sexual contact, they may actually be asking for intimacy

---

[63] Harvard's Health Beat archive, November 22, 2011. http://www.health.harvard.edu/healthbeat/giving-thanks-can-make-you-happier

[64] You Just Don't Understand, by Deborah Tannen, is one of the best books I've ever read about communication style differences. Her book is binary-gendered, but still very valuable because most people have one communication style or the other.

and closeness--they may be asking for a way back into the relationship's best stuff. If a partner is the other way around, and wants to feel close prior to sex, try not to see it as a rejection or as a lack of desire for connection from them, but instead understand this style difference and see what they need to feel close before getting physical.

Conclusion

Saying Yes to our partners' love can have a profound effect on our relationships. When they feel appreciated, it not only makes them feel good about themselves, it also makes them feel good about us and about the relationship or marriage. All of these are separate pleasures and satisfactions that we all need. We want our partners to be happy. We need to hear that they are happy, and that we have a role in that. Having said this, it's vitally important that we offer the same to them by receiving the love that they give, by letting them know that we see it, and by expressing happiness and appreciation for their giving.

When we say Yes to love, we say Yes to our own happiness. And, when we are happy, others around us are happier, as well.

CHAPTER 16
THE DEEP YES

Yes is an attitude, a stance, a paradigm but mainly, it is a practice. It is not merely positive thinking, or abundance consciousness, or openness, or mindfulness, though it includes all of these. Yes is an active taking in. It is the moment that you take to look into the eyes of a loved one or a stranger, and you absorb the love or concern that they have for you.

As a practice, the simplest part of this is to breathe. When we see something beautiful, when we hear something wonderful, when we feel something exquisite, when we experience something fascinating, when we taste something delectable, when we catch the scent of something fragrant, breathe it in. Take a breath, take a moment, and fully receive. The littlest things, practiced over time, are always the most transformative.

No matter how you may choose to use the practices in this book or your own Deep Yes practice, know that the Yes you practice is not only good for you, it is important in and for the world. The more that we take in, in a healthy way, the more that we can set a balance in the world's energy. A healthy, deep Yes means we need less because we consume less in order to be satisfied, and this is good for the planet.

A healthy Yes is a healthy Yin. When Yin is healthy, the Yang, our outgoing energy, also balances. This is good news for everyone. No more pushing. Instead we simply move forward joyfully. This means less violence, less chasing after things, and more true and beautiful initiative.

Readers of this book, those of you who have gotten all the way here to the end, I wish you joy. I wish you success. I wish you all of the happiness, health and life that the practice of a Deep Yes contains. I hope that we meet up at some point and you can share some of your Yes experiences with me. Until then--say Yes!!

41725424R00087

Made in the USA
Middletown, DE
21 March 2017